Contrapuntos IX

❖

Antropoceno

Lacie Rae Cunningham, ed.
Marcos Pico Rentería, ed.

DIGITUS
INDIE PUBLISHERS

EDITORES INDEPENDIENTES
Monterey, CA

Diseño · *Design:* Mariam Karbassi & Marcos Pico Rentería

Editor: Marcos Pico Rentería
Guest Editor: Lacie Rae Cunningham

First print edition: 2022

ISBN Digitus Indie Publishers: 978-0-9982539-5-4

ISSN 2 4 7 2 - 2 0 6 5 (print)
ISSN 2 4 7 2 - 2 0 7 3 (online)
www.digitusindie.com

ÍNDICE
CONTENTS

NARRATIVA

88

RESEÑA
123

AUTORES
134

INTRO

ANTROPOCENO

IT USED TO BE A SIMPLE FORMULA: the writer, the reader, each with his own precision made the calculation of the perfect environment to commit to a page. Close your eyes; a dark cornered café, a clean studio desk, the metro, the coast, an indie bookstore basement workshop, a covered forest. Simply put, whoever you are, dear reader / writer, we expect something of the world around us to provide a ritualistic space for literary traditions.

The decision to hail this edition as *Antropoceno*, a word evoking environment and destruction, recognizes that the mapping out of these spaces is asking a bit more of us now.

Pleistocene, Holocene, Anthropocene, Chthulucene, Capital-ocene, to name a few, are terms developed (and debated) in an attempt to question the possibilities of a *before and after, surviving and perishing*. It is intertwined with threads of ontological upsets, interspecies livelihoods, and coalescences of contagions and contaminations. In our current moment, the 'where' of our creative and lived spaces becomes othered. Will it be inside or outside, before or after, distance and dying, reside. *Antropoceno*, carries with it messages of doom, survival, profound loss, and renewal visualized through trans-disciplinary cooperation. I defer to Donna Haraway's contact zones to underscore how we are constituted relationally.

The new edition of Contrapuntos *Antropoceno* aptly falls under the number IX. As one reads this text, he/she/they will be anticipating toward X, the unexpected, the precarious, what I would call the looping of the 'relative' and the 'relato.' The curation of *Antropoceno* collaborates with a range of artists as a collective and intimate act.

Beginning from the outside, Visual Artist Mariam Karbassi's Luchadores Tristes pays homage to his encounter with a familial COVID bereavement as visualizing masculine grief. As the reader opens the book, it provides permission to recognize what the present has done to our environment and as an invitation step through this ninth edition's literary door to see what has been created during our great inside/outside shift and the distance between us.

POESÍA: abounds in and energizes *Antropoceno,* caressing both pessimistic and playful. To file into the inauguration of this work, consider Natalia Chamorro's offering, "que volver a la poesía / es como salir al balcón / en cuarentena / es volar in situ / mientras llegas a la ventana más lejana" to Lordan's "Lockdown Animals" clamouring that "Since lockdown began / feral cats come closer each day / to licking or biting my hand" or the betwixt and between of Rodrigo Toscano's diablito Mardi Gras who is more party-yet animal and in his subsequent poem rifled with tragic Bestia cadavers. The authors recede and doubly manage to bring the reader back into a center. It recalls Gaia theory--what is heterogeneous yet coherent.

NARRATIVA: seasoned with a similar push and pull. Entries include stories of speculative ill-fated Earthlings and wastelands (Ewa Mazierska) to fantasies of another kind in "El tour del amor" (Francisco Díaz Klaassen). This is Anthropocene's twin flame Chthulucene, a recognition of sympoetic composition of a common world in very much living and also very much dying.

RESEÑA: because libraries and academia will never become extinct. *Erótica* never hurt anyone; the short stories and vignettes are grounded in a canonical past / present intra-history. The anchor of this book is a review of Blues Castellano/Castilian Blues if rife with the execution of recall and memory. Thus, will end this diatribe with a return to the query of a *before and after* resurface in this closing section as it is reflected in the premise of *Antropoceno IX.*

INSTRUCTIONS: Reader/writer: navigate a disastrous and brilliant present, embark upon catastrophic future-tripping, and may this collection serve as a field guide for un-calculating, for rethinking the spaces we occupy as they are acutely refracted in the following chapters.

POESÍA

ALGÚN DÍA EN ABRIL

Natalia Chamorro

CON LETRA CHIQUITA
de huellas de pájaro
para que no vea mi lado derecho
cómo subo
a mi arca personal

que volver a la poesía
es como salir al balcón
en cuarentena
es volar in situ
mientras llegas a la ventana más lejana
reconoces una sombra
ves que te saluda
y ahora sabes que existe y te esperará
al día siguiente
y para siempre
aunque el día este oscuro
y la lluvia

que no parará en cada día contra ti
limpiará quien eras, te preguntas
¿quién será la que baje a la ciudad
y se pierda en la autopista y la distancia?
que sean estos días navegando
contra el diluvio para nada,
temes
que no te de miedo escribir
que los pájaros te despiertan
cada mañana
de primavera a verano

y que aquí

en el balcón
respiras un vuelo alto

y que los tordos cantan para ti
a bordo del arca

PATAS ARRIBA

Natalia Chamorro

ENTRÓ UNA CUCARACHA GIGANTE
todas lo son
el miedo es
evitar caminar por donde ha pasado
y muerto
patas arriba
en este corto espacio
en mi refugio y
casi a mi lado

ahora
ya no puedo
caminar sin zapatos
ya se arruinó el espacio donde podía
estar cerca de algo y
no pensar en las distancias

ahora vive la urgencia
de voltear la mirada
y descubrirla a mi lado

el miedo es rápido
por eso me sorprende saber que
ya estaba medio muerta
cuando se metió a la casa

habrá llegado enferma de la calle

EL AHORCADO I

Yasef Ananda

IRIS DE SOMBRAS CHINESCAS
incienso para el muerto que se inventa
su tarde elemental

amanecerá (sin sueño)
un aprendiz de haikú por cuenta propia

Ser el ahorcado tiene sus privilegios inmortales

THE HANGED MAN I

Yasef Ananda
Translated by Erika Bondi

IRIS OF CHINESE SHADOWS
Incense for the dead that make up
their own primordial afternoon

He will wake (not drowsy)
an apprentice of haiku by his own account

Being the hanged man has its immortal privileges

DISONANCIA

Yasef Ananda

BOCETÓ LA FURTIVA DIMENSIÓN
que la palabra encarna
y los músculos obedecieron

Extrañamiento que borra de golpe
los designios de dios
como la ola a la arena en roca firme

DISSONANCE

Yasef Ananda
Translated by Erika Bondi

HE SKETCHED THE FURTIVE DIMENSION
that the word incarnates
and the muscles obeyed

Estrangement that suddenly erases
the will of god
like the sand waves on bedrock

TRISTEZA

Consuelo Hernández

¿A DÓNDE SE FUERON TUS JARDINES
mi amada tacita de plata?
¿tu eterna primavera
tus calles para correr sin miedo
el aire limpio y tus flores amarillas?

¿Dónde tu lluvia de alegrías
el viento prodigioso
desordenando el cabello de muchachos
sin mente de cuchillos, ni golpes, ni pistolas?

¿Dónde tus estrellas diurnas
los colibríes amigos,
los padres protectores
y la hermosa locura de artistas y poetas?

¿Por qué los pájaros enfermos expuestos a las hondas
madres masticando pavimento
ofreciendo sus hijas al mejor postor
niñas aspirando sacol y gasolina
engalanando sus horas sin abrigo
sin padres...
sin amor?

La ciudad estaba herida
y con toda esta vida que se fue
a plena luz del día, brotaron mis lágrimas
frente al parque, en el atrio de la catedral.

SADNESS

Consuelo Hernández

.

WHERE HAVE YOUR GARDENS GONE
my beloved city bright as a new pin?
Your perpetual spring
your streets to run down without fear
your refreshing air, your yellow flowers?

Where your rainfall of joys
the prodigious breeze
ruffling the hair of boys
with thoughts far from knives, fists and guns?

Where your daytime stars
friendly hummingbirds,
protective parents
and the beautiful madness of artists and poets?

Why ailing birds exposed to slingshots
anguished mothers on the sidewalk
offering their daughters to the highest bidder
young girls sniffing glue and gasoline
dressing up their hours with no shelter
with no parents...
with no love?

The city was wounded
and with all this life that disappeared
in broad daylight, I burst into tears
in the cathedral's atrium, facing the park.

SUEÑOS EN FUGA

Consuelo Hernández

COMO LUCIÉRNAGAS NOS BEBEMOS LA LUNA
por avenidas de asfalto retorcidas
soñamos con playas vírgenes
con amaneceres ebrios y una luz más cierta...

Añoramos el canto de la fuente
la espesa siembra
y una fogata para ahuyentar el tigre.

Los bosques de clorofila alborozada
ya no sostienen el vuelo de las aves
exiliados del solaz diurno del paisaje
de la canción del viento entre las ramas.

Nos queda la fiebre del planeta
la nostalgia del verde,
los sueños en fuga
los laberintos de concreto
como su hervidero de hormigas voraces
                    que devora la selva...

DREAMS IN FLIGHT

Consuelo Hernández

LIKE FIREFLIES WE DRINK UP THE MOON
along paved crooked streets
dreaming of virgin beaches
and inebriated sunrises with clearer light...

We miss the fountain's song
the dense planting
and a bonfire to scare off tigers.

The forests of exultant chlorophyll
no longer sustain the flight of birds
exiled from the daily solace of landscape
from wind songs streaming through branches.

We're left with high fever on the planet
nostalgia for greenery,
dreams in flight
and concrete labyrinths
like a swarm of voracious ants
                                    devouring the jungle...

LLUVIA EN LA AMAZONIA

Consuelo Hernández

VINO OTRA VEZ LA LLUVIA A CÁNTAROS
 incesantemente riega la tarde.

Protegida por un techo de palma en el escampadero
estoy en la gran altura de Macedonia
conversando con una mujer miraña, un ticuna
  y un huitoto...
  tres naciones indígenas
  y bajo el inmenso cielo, se desliza el Amazonas.

Iluminan los relámpagos
caen rayos y la lluvia moja
y persiste un temor de cruzar a la casa
con sabor a caracoles y anémonas...
Cae la noche
el agua lleva los troncos en silencio
hojas de palma, basura, aves muertas
y reflotan recuerdos que creíamos olvidados...

Cambia de ritmo la lluvia
goterones fuertes...
el silencio refresca sin mojarnos...
La enorme hoja de yautía es un paraguas
para descender de la cima
bañados de alegría limpia
brillamos con la luz de la sonrisa pura
y caminamos hasta la casa de la indígena
con el huitoto desconfiado que ha perdido su inocencia.

Llegamos
la lluvia cesa
y somos fruto nuevo,
una gota,
un caimán

un cocodrilo...
todo y nada
después de este purificador baño pluvial.

RAIN IN THE AMAZON

Consuelo Hernández

RAIN CAME POURING DOWN AGAIN
ceaselessly showering the afternoon.

Protected by the shelter's palm-thatched roof
in Macedonia's great heights
I am chatting with a Miraña woman, a Ticuna
    and a Huitoto man...
     three original nations
     and under the immense sky, the Amazon ambles along.

Lightning flashes
rays crash and rain soaks
and we're afraid to run down to the house
with its smell of snails and anemones...
Night falls
water silently carries branches
palm fronds, trash, dead birds
and floating memories that we thought long-forgotten.

The rain shifts its rhythm
large, heavy drops...
without soaking us, the silence refreshes...
The broad yautia leaf is my umbrella
as we descend from the peak
bathed in clean joy
shining with the light of a pure smile
walking to the home of the native woman
with the distrustful Huitto who lost his innocence.

We arrive
the rain stops
and we are new fruit,
a raindrop,
an alligator

a crocodile...
all and nothing
after this purifying pluvial bath.

PROPIEDAD PRIVADA

Consuelo Hernández

TODO SE LO LLEVARON LOS SEÑORES DEL PODER
los desarrollistas enrollaron el paisaje en su ambición
los inversores invirtieron los valores
los interesados se desinteresaron por el prójimo.

Tierra violada
erosionados tus montes
contaminada tu leche curativa
herida tu piel de mujer.

Ya no habrá playas para ti
             mi niño
no habrá aire limpio en tu paisaje
la tierra ya tiene dueños
el oxígeno y el agua tienen dueños
y hoy leí en el diario que se subasta
             la luz del astro rey...

Debes construir un refugio
             en el fondo de tu ser
y aprender a vivir del resplandor de tu propia desnudez.

PRIVATE PROPERTY

Consuelo Hernández

THOSE IN POWER TOOK EVERYTHING
ambitious developers ruined the landscape
investors inverted our values
those interested in their neighbors got detached.

Violated Earth
your mountains eroded
your healing milk contaminated
your woman's skin wounded.

No more beaches for you
                my child
there won't be clean air in your sphere
the Earth has owners now
oxygen and water have owners
and today in the paper I read that
              sunlight is up for auction...

You should build a refuge
              at the depths of your being
and learn how to live from the radiance of your own nudity.

LEY NATURAL

Consuelo Hernández

IMPROVISACIÓN
                    desorden...
el futuro no tiene forma asegurada
lo inscribes cada día de tu vida
en las calles
entre la copa de magnolias
en las luces de neón
en el texto de tus redes sociales.

Un nuevo libreto fraguas cada segundo
cuando danzas
mueves el mundo,
                    matrix para cambiar monotonías
para fijar nuevos trazos
y cartografías inéditas...

En la ciudad que transitas
                    todo cambia
la naturaleza señorea
                    destrona
vuelve humildes a los orgullosos
                    doblega
                    detiene
a los que van a contracorriente en carrera desbocada
porque las leyes de natura no se alimentan de cuentos.

NATURAL LAW

Consuelo Hernández

IMPROVISATION
    chaos....
the future has no defined shape
you inscribe it each day of your life
on the streets
in magnolia treetops
in glowing neon lights
in texts on your social networks.

A new script you forge every second
when you dance
you move the world,
   matrix to break monotonies
setting new lines
and undisclosed cartographies...

In the city you are crossing
    all is changing
nature is sovereign
    dethrones
turns the proud humble
    dominates
    halts
those who dash countercurrent in a runaway race
because the laws of nature are not fueled by tales.

Note: translations in English by Consuelo Hernández & Maria Roof.

IN THE QUARRELSOME SEA

J. J. Steinfeld

IN THE QUARRELSOME SEA
perhaps a storm is beginning to stretch its emotions
perhaps the calmness is trickery
you forget the words for swimming and drowning
you lose track of time and concepts
you neglect the past and ignore the future
it is the water that it the language
if not of God than of the sea itself
God and the sea speak on equal terms
in debate and in love and in humour
you fail to understand anything
except the water as water
and God as God
but you make an effort
a strong, wilful effort
to recall the definitions
of swimming and drowning.

START BY COUNTING
THE GRAINS OF SAND

J. J. Steinfeld

HOW MUCH DO YOU NEED TO KNOW
to be free in this life?
Can you embrace freedom
without knowing the names of birds?
Without recognizing the intent of insects?
Without breathing in uncomplicated mysteries?
Can you escape
the doom of the body's treachery
without a mastery of words?
Can you negotiate with God
in silence and with empty pockets?
Can you feast
upon the ordinary and everyday
without touching the lucidity of animals?
The tides, the sunrises, phases of the moon—
can you comprehend without despairing
unknowing and unconcerned?
Storms, absence of storms, sunsets—
can you make calculations of love
inward and hands against ears?

The first question again
repeated as a slap to the senses:
How much do you need to know
to be free in this life?
Start by counting the grains of sand
slowly, one at a time,
overwhelmed by joy.

the police officer taking the information
for the missing-person's report
looked somewhat like an owl
and you mention that
but too softly for anyone to hear.

THE LANGUAGE
OF THE NATURAL WORLD

J. J. Steinfeld

AS I WAS RUNNING BY THE SOFT-SPOKEN RIVER
a fish called to me
I don't get your poetry
it makes my swimming
go in a lopsided direction
but if I wrote poetry
the talkative fish said
you would be one of my metaphors
right in the first or second stanza
of a beautifully fishy poem.

I began to run faster
as if articulate fish
were the flowing cause
of fear and speed.

I've been thinking a great deal
of love and heartbreak
and the end of the world
said a second fish
larger and with an unwatery accent
unlike the first
that sounded watery
if not downright erudite.

As I continued to run
past the soft-spoken river
and into the loveliest
of whispering forests
how I am glad
angry forest beasts
can't speak
all that articulately.

NOT LIKE SOIL AND WATER AND AIR

J. J. Steinfeld

YOU'VE BEEN NOTIFIED BY GOD AND YOUR EMPLOYER
that you're not all that necessary
not like soil and water and air.

What is old, you want to say,
the earth, the sun, the galaxy
the oldest particle in existence
the oldest thought
the oldest belief
the oldest person who still thinks about sex?
This is what you were thinking, somewhat,
as you were being given the heave-ho,
the golden handshake by God is squeezed too hard
you search for images for your pain
the divine kiss-off by employer leaves you wiping your lips
you search for a towel to dry your despair.

All your life, you realize,
like being notified that your illness is more serious
than first thought,
that you haven't asked enough questions
and you vow to begin soon
as soon as you compile the list
in order of least to most profound
you clear your throat, have a sip of water
that same necessary water contemplated before
in the reach of God and your employer
and ask away, as if your life depended on the asking.

IN THIS DARKEST OF FORESTS
AT NIGHTFALL

J. J. Steinfeld

LIGHTNING OR DECAY? I WONDER,
not realizing my thoughts could be so clear
in this darkest of forests at nightfall.

I was toppled for sadness
because I could not imagine love
as well as I used to.

Closer I inspected the majestic tree
this toppled mind-reader.
Roots, branches, age rings
analogous to what? I say aloud.

I don't need to speak words
I am my words and thoughts.

I need to speak if I desire to be
I respond in inconclusive argument.

What words will you offer
as I turn to memory?

I believe that God prays to you
even toppled in the rumour of eternity
in this darkest of forests at nightfall.

Your observations are questionable
too unnatural for forest darkness.
As for me in my toppled state:
no subterfuge, no feigned dreaming
no need for falsehoods or disbelief—
now leave my place of dying.

I attempt words of farewell
and find myself speechless.

THE LANDSCAPE FALTERS, LOST MEANINGS RE-EMERGE

J. J. Steinfeld

I HAVE A SECRET TO SHARE WITH YOU
(maybe not a secret, more like a contradiction
or a blundering confession)
something I learned in the artificial light
of anxiety and reshaping lost selves.

Well, you see, hope is infinite
hopelessness is thin as a knife blade
against your throat on a sun-filled day
the only thing that makes absolute sense
is senselessness and its cunning attendants.

The landscape falters, lost meanings re-emerge,
I'm still offering words and re-made dreams
with a flaw of archaeology occurring
in the terrain between truth and deception.

And the question remains
who will fall in first,
the one who reveals
or the one who hears
or both unceremoniously together?

AS HIDDEN ANIMALS OBSERVE ME

J. J. Steinfeld

ANOTHER MISPLACED EVENING
of wandering the woods
darkness growing
as hidden animals
observe me with caution
and bemusement.

What have you noticed today?
a small sullen voice asks.
*Be careful where you place
your exclamation marks
and bold underlining,*
a loud cheery voice warns.
*Devour love before
love devours you,*
a loveless voice instructs.

I look around for the voices
rather, the source of the words,
noticing nothing, heeding no one,
then fall to the ground
before I take flight
to the clouds
so I can better notice
what I have missed.

PAUSE

Sreekanth Kopuri

MY BULLOCK CART OF
golden mangos still
rests beside the road

tired of the silence the
death angel burns to
paralyse time's nerves

in my brother's lost hope
his body hangs in his noodle
shop near the haloed church –

a message that life will never
be the same again, but with
weird pauses to break, out in

the Mumbai red light, heaps of
emptiness in hollowed bowls
of prostitutes fill their days, and

the grandeur of the largest democracy
is dwarfed by the government's blind
deafness to the migrants' public funerals.

FLOWERS

Sreekanth Kopuri

WHEN SWAY THEIR HEADS,
greet us with the wind's
language in our eyes to
connect the unknown to
the known buds of our
stunted language, we are
always elsewhere where
the hands of time leaf
the pages off our calendars
burning them in the tongues
of those flaming night shifts
in the air-conditioned cells
flowering counter flowers
against the earth's weedy
impulses muted under our feet.

A COVID EVENING

Sreekanth Kopuri

a letter from India

OF WEIRD SILENCE
heavy without
footprints to walk
this into another sun

but the fickle sky's
changing colors in
its drunken face
pretend searching

meanings, to flee our
anger hidden in our
startled eyes that peep
only from behind the

quarantined hope, I
trespass to touch this
twilight where our
clay Gods too pray,

fast as their customers
are fired, off now our
hypertense dreams search
for a future that waits in

some Nobel laureate's
vaccinated idea but here
since the time's lost in the
thistly grip of dragon's claws

I dare hold it and stroll
ahead into the hidden
meanings - the hunger
of four mongrels unpack

over a lost calf that searches
its future in the dried up
garbage heap, its last pulse
charges at them as a

police whistle scatters
all the roads we quit are
stalked by the vulturous
eyeballs that wait to

hold our throats to suck
our voices into their
unfathomed silence, a
sudden shriek of a doctor's

family breaks, down the church
street where the Eid Salah calls
for the answer that distances from
a son's silence after his tears dry up

when the civic staff remove his
father's death by an earth mover
moving the earth we see only on
the quarantined little screens.

VOICE OF A FOETUS

Sreekanth Kopuri

from a garbage heap, Machilipatnam

I'M THE RIPENING FRUIT
of desire in you.

I know I'm not the sun
that will rise above the mountains

of your hope tomorrow but you know
there are hands in the world that wait for me.

Life isn't in the garbage heaps
nor in a pack of stray dogs.

My unknown fathers disown me.
So, let me cry a cry of hope
before it recedes into silence.

GANESH RITUAL

Sreekanth Kopuri

SRIDEVI WRAPS THE GRACEFUL FOLDS
of autumn's rippling smile around
her golden texture, in saffron sari,
an offering to the dark naked clay
Ganesha, the autumn-born belly
god, marks the seasonal sanctity
at the door, steps into the lush
guava orchard, plucks the ripe
dreams smiling green on the
Ganseh chaturthi pandal that
bears the season's mellowing
hope in the parrot-green elephant
apples and the incense wisps of
her burning piety with a mousy
humility, around which the radiant
circles of her devout hope halo
the natural wisdom that the earth
gives as the four-armed elephantine
providence of the creation.

PERMANENCIA DE LOS OBJETOS

Lucía Orellana Damacela

AMARILLO QUEMADO INTENSO
mi sol interior
con rosas fucsia
máculas
dibujadas a mano
jarrón chino
de forma redonda
cuya información
de manufactura
me tradujo la dueña de la tienda
en el revés del recibo

no va con el resto
de la casa pero soy incapaz
de deshacerme de él
quién compraría un jarrón chino
tan poco tradicional
tan soy quien soy y ya
tan descarado
al final me gusta
me interroga
la primera pregunta
siendo
por qué diablos lo compré

a mi espalda
la musa ecológica
ojos y ramas
un grabado
prueba de artista
de un ecuatoriano
de firma ilegible

por el espacio
entre mi hombro
y mi cabeza
el jarrón y la eco musa
escrutan mis escritos
mis palabras encriptadas
en solidez virtual

los objetos
a mi alrededor
despiden más polvo
que antes
y así me hablan
me piden atención
emanan memorias
residuos
que danzan con la luz

artefactan mi historia
y atrapada en este
mausoleo ornamentado
los objetos más mínimos
[la pequeña escultura
de una pareja sosteniendo
a un bebé
cuya base se rompió
y reparé hace algunos años]
[el plato de cristal
azul transluciente
muy diminuto para el espacio
del que está a cargo pero igual]
se vuelven estridentes
resuenan entre las paredes
como si cada momento
que representan de mi vida
durara para siempre
como si el tiempo rehusara
moverse y se hubiera convertido
en una gelatina incolora
que debo atravesar para alcanzar
mis palabras mis objetos

THE SCIENCE OF STORYTELLING

John Madera

"I start in the middle of a
sentence and move both
directions at once."
—John Coltrane

CALL IT A CHARACTER flaw, but I did not read your essay on how I can
[create
characters with unique and interesting flaws that lead into plots that will

enliven my stories, because I, too, woke up to the sad news of Umberto Eco
[dying
today at eighty-four, when he died over four years ago in Milan. How
dreadful to die

again! Is there a prima materia of which all language is composed?
I am listening to Miles Davis right now and reveling in all the so-called

flaws: the clams and fracks and burps and splutters. The gaps
is   what
music   means.
Can I just say "aporia" and "contingency" and have them mean? Probably

not. I hate the locution "asking for a friend." And, yes, I have fallen
into the hellhole of a tweet considering how the Karen's day started.

Yes, maybe her mother had died. Maybe she'd discovered her husband
was having an affair. The all-caps of people sometimes having bad days.

Etcetera. I've had bad days but not once have I tried to have someone
lynched. You diminish jazz when you describe it as the evil empire's

"classical music," the categorization diminishing its anarchic qualia
in favor of its so-called democratic expressions. Criticism without

affect is history without multiplicity and therefore dead. A poem is

48

a lexical appoggiatura. Hear Davis's finger-snapped lead-in to "Love

for Sale," the gentle crispness of it. Hear Evans's displacements of space,
the architectonics of delay, of caesura, of breathing. Two-and-a-half
minutes

of anticipation and it sounds like hours, hours of desire, hours of love,
which, by definition, always exists outside of the marketplace: death.

Which is to say, the social media app partially muted my video because
it may contain music that belongs to someone else, said someone else

perhaps living musicked in Andorra, United Arab Emirates, Afghanistan,
Antigua and Barbuda, Anguilla, or one hundred fifty-nine other countries.

No contagion deaths were registered in Milan, in all of Lombardy,
yesterday and today, and so large crowds crowd bars; and Virgil

joins them but they can't see him sitting in a dark corner inventing
a new eclogue: a poetics of urban disturbance; can't see Caravaggio

attending to the moment's ongoing visceral tenebroso, can't see Monteverdi
inking white pages into black constellations. Nightlife? Life is always night.

TWO SPACES AFTER A PERIOD

John Madera

"PERDIDO" is in the air and it is a pleasing disturbance, and
I am wondering if they are wondering, like I am wondering,
if someone or something is missing or has gone missing or
they are not where I expect them to be and I cannot find them.

All this talk about flying away makes me wonder, "If there is a city
of angels, then there is a city of devils" and "If there is a city
of angels and a city of devils, then there must be a city
of ghosts," where every day is an escape, every night a citadel.

I am in this room, in this city, where every breath is a question mark,
every look, cloacal, every sound, massy, where every day is
the day before: a La Monte Young composition on infinite repeat,
a Béla Tarr film looped, a brick of a book you brag about not having

read, but nights—after day's frenzies, travesties, intensities—lost,
after hours addressing errors "establishing a database connection,"
hours trying but failing to connect with anything, or anyone,
any of my friends and family, failing to address anything, really,

I wonder if something exists, someone exists, somewhere
exists, by its absence, by their absence, whether or not
he or she or they or it are in the room, the space around the object,
the space around the subject, as much object as the missing object,

as much subject as the missing subject, or maybe I'm missing
something, like when I'm outside, pretending to be missing,
a phantom haunting the city, streets and buildings and cars
ghosts themselves, rain a massive beaded curtain, the wind

rending apart my umbrella, reducing its ribbing to a ruined
but sparkling spiderweb, and a ghost from a fraud service center
calls to say they "detected" "suspicious activity" on my card,
to say I might be somewhere where I wasn't: buying gas when I don't

even have a car, which makes me suspect being here and being
not there makes me suspect, a suspect, something for some sleuth

to figure out, while I reconcile the mundane and the bizarre,
the everyday of every day with every day's turbulence,

alarum, bedlam, while I realize the world has another brain,
one I can't yet puzzle out, has another heart, our pulses
slowly synchronizing, like pendulum clocks talking
to each other, their ticking transferring minute amounts

of energy, minutes eventually swinging together,
collapsing the whatever it was separating them,
maybe the thing Matisse, who didn't paint things,
painted: the "difference between things," the smog.

LOCKDOWN ANIMALS

Dave Lordan

ACCORDING TO THE LEAFLET
rats are all over our estate
especially the bin units.

According to RTE
billions of huge flying Ants
are swarming from the east.

I saw several weeks ago
black cat Shadow swallow
two Yellowtits whole & raw.

Since lockdown began
feral cats come closer each day
to licking or biting my hand.

The hedgehog in my neighbour's garden
is without peace since
its discovery by children.

DISCLOSURE

Dave Lordan

I SAW THEM
down by the bay

two young lovers strolling
hand in hand

towards the overgrown lane
past that ancient graffiti

as if the world
had not changed

as if such things
as young lovers

beelining down
overgrown lanes

past ancient graffiti
were still proper

still possible
in the new times

under the new laws.
I saw them and

I regret to say
I did not report them.

I told no-one about them, til now.

THE MAN WITH NO MASK

Dave Lordan

WHEN, FOLLOWING THE BIG WIN- THE REAL BIGGIE-
uncountable zeros after his name-
he stands his friends an endless reservoir of stout
and decrees every church
a twenty-four-hour shebeen

abolishes retching and reflux and coughs
plugs the ancient flow of anal bleeding
decrees the removal of sleep from the brain
and promises the people that none
need ever stop drinking and smoking and snorting
and gambling and chomping ever again.

Ten-million-year weekend begins.
The paralytic age.
Then. Something mighty
cracks in the head of the Chieftain of Chiefs,
an unquenchable surging of rage through the blood
that cometary rage at being
not the only God

and off he goes to war against the world
grinding armies to dust
drowning archipelagos
hurling mountains into the sun

New York falls to him
and then the whole of Scotland
then Bangkok, Bhutan, Yakutsk.

Finalé – his incredible one-man stampede,
two legs tied behind, routing
Skibbereen and Stalingrad, the Black and Tans, the Vietcong
and Mossad.

Every last man jack of 'em.
Bored and still mad up for it,
he announces a gang resurrection
bringing back to the mainland of clay and despair
Georgie Best and Michael Collins,
Christy Ring and Elvis.

One by one, in headlines everywhere,
he completely defeats them
at soccer and handball and hurling and dancing
at head-the-ball, bare knuckle fisting, cock-fights
and freaking out women.

Whereupon he finally declares himself
the Permanent Champion Of Everything.

Then, to end and begin, outstretched,
he assumpts himself live onstage in Moonshine Stadium
kaleidoscopically spinning
fountaining fireworks

as he bends to show off
a shining New Ireland
emerging from his a-ho like an egg.

STICKS

Dave Lordan

ARE THE TREE'S SPROUT, BUT THE WIND'S GIFT.
I choose the straightest among what I pluck
from the briars
      or the shade by the ditch;

hip-height and thumb-thick and bone-strong.

I won't take one too gluey with resin.
I won't take one too old and too parched and too likely to crack.

A whorling gnarl
half a hand
from the thick end
will give a
good grip.

There is one imperative. Presumably it's God's.
Or the sky's
      or the bog's
          or the wind's.

The wind is the voice of the sky saying this:
A branch is not a stick
and snapping off a healthy branch
will draw a heavy curse on life.
What and where cannot be said.
A healthy branch is a well of dread.

Still, ancient impulse leans to the perfect bond of a stick.
I feel a far ancestral honouring.

I shake the stick above my head and yawp like Eve,
yawp like Rousseau, yawp as beardy Whitman did.

     and rise   and rise
I fall   and fall
and twist in my own yawping stick-dance,

spiralling to archetypal dreamtime,
to distant eidolons of human wilderness;
a million years old and unexpelled,
not yet parted from the forest...

....romantic guff,
paint and fumes to cheat my guilt, deny reality.
For God is only living-life, and when I was eight I tortured God,
tormented animals, hacked at sapping wood.

At eight a boy's already part of teak,
already animated by his stick;
his spear,
       his wand,
            his staff,
                 his rod.

Each battling phantom in his DNA
still grasping through the aeons
at this multi-purpose limb,

this cable routing him
through instant ages up
to modern man,

to man who'd slash a path through anything,
to man who stands back to probe
without touching,

to man who handles the world
without feeling,

to man by which the hacked tree sows
its Amazon of grief,

to man by which the numb roots spread
colonising every nerve and tip.

I am man now, and I'm getting a grip.

DRIFT

Irene Cooper

[CONFLUENCE/DIVERGENCE]

hydrologic sponge of volcanic bedrock
feeds the river of falls
which joins the Crooked and
                    Metolius at Billy Chinook
reservoir is French for keep, Old English for hold
but nothing holds. under our slow eye
rock yawns and stretches at our feet
                    in geologic terms
it's only a minute or so since lava flowed
and cooled to form the porous basin that seizes
and draws the rain from run off
                    watery keep sinks, circulates
emerging months and years ahead as spring
          unless it doesn't. Whychus Creek, old
steelhead paradise saw none nor no Chinook
for fifty years and more
                              peculiar
web of waterways and stable
diverted to dry and dire straits
               what if there was yoga for rivers,
an asana to raise the winter flow from its score
of cubic feet per second,
                    gentle the summer floods
raise all boats and restore
the nimble reaches to their hardy oddities

[bas(in) nature]

jay bathes in a sprinkler-puddled swing
lawn mower stirs a doe to lift her gaze

coyote cruises Deschutes River Woods at noon
at twilight, bucks leap like sk8rboyz on Colorado

black bear paws Tumalo Creek,
moony racoon wakes the chickens, riles the dogs

vixen skitters her red kits across highway 97
sudden owl swoops before the headlights

bobcat skims the dusty rimrock
sights us, surprises us on our careful trails

[greater sage grouse]

they numbered 16 million 50 years or so ago
and today the rough count's 500K, plenty
to grouse about for the living three percent, plus uncrushed
        species that swim the sagebrush sea:
pygmy rabbits, pronghorn, golden eagles, coyote;
yellow bells, milkvetch, tarweed fiddleneck,
—350 entities native to the brush
        a lek is the place male grouse display their moves,
spike the air with punk fans of tailfeathers, puff their masculine air
            [sacs,
gloop gloop. sage chickens mating on the sage steppe
losing ground and cover fast to fire, juniper creep,
people. in Oregon, at least, the ranchers are onboard:
        save the bird, save the herd
across state lines, nothing rhymes with gas, with oil
but back to sex: the choreography commences at golden dawn,
competitive and feathered as any rodeo
    many are called to the ancient do-si-do, few get to do the deed
lonely males await their season in a patch of scrub
females get busy with the babies
    the grouse is not endangered, per se, but we watch,

we watch, this bellwether, this indicator, we watch,
tick tock, the canary as it dances in the coal mine

[river critters]

macroinvertebrates lack a spine
& are nimble environmental indicators of:
nutrient availability
temperature
oxygen levels:
the ethereal dragonfly, the lowly flatworm
eco-mates to the macrolepidopteran:
swallowtail butterfly at the Metolius
gothic window paned splendor, red ombres to gold to coolish black

hatch chart in January:
 mayfly in slack slow water and back eddies
 caddis in deep slow runs
 the stone fly, the midge—in April they're in the riffles, the soft
                                             [runs, the tail-outs
in May the salmon fly risk the fast and heavy boulder runs
fish only want what anybody in their position would:
a gravel bottom
calm backwaters
side channels
—& for hiding,
deep pools
sunk debris

declared a threatened species in 2014, the spotted frog
has it rough—no wetland in winter, eggs flushed downstream in
                                                    [summer
makes it hard to get a jump on the whole survival thing

a spot can be a blemish—or
a spot can be a fixed point on the horizon
a way to focus

[straight]

WANING

Ellen Sander

EACH DAY, LIGHT FADES EARLIER
and we, the animals, the geranium, the balding apple tree
grow more tired, with a perfect weariness, the bend
of bones as they lie down in age.

Decay, transition, anticipation of
snow, wither switchgrass on the shouldered fieldf.
Comes then a softness of collapse, surrender, slow
heaving of the earth's gold-lit bow.

Light lies lower in the sky, velveting shadows on the moss.
Moist brown leaves paste to my shoe in the wet morning as
the dog and I amble the road with ground
fog and scatters of birdcall.

ADRIFT

Róger Lindo
Translated by Matthew Byrne

I.

AND HERE I AM
in a simple attempt
so the hurricane
can take my place
in the fight to stay on my feet

May it drag me
far away
one lone wave
to a space
without coordinates

I am the current
and the limbo

II.

The same wave
deposited our bones
on this beach

Time to stand
clamber
light a fire
feel the innocent naïvité
of the labyrinth

One morning
I decided to make myself anew
adrift

APPLE TREE

Colin Ian Jeffery

THERE IS AN APPLE TREE, OLD AND GNARLED
At the bottom of my garden, again in bloom
On which in childhood my brother and I played
Climbing high and low, swinging on branches
Laughing, so full of fun, chasing each other
Loving, and enjoying each other's company.
Sweet memories of a brother long dead
Dying of heart-attack in his sixty-first year.
Tree, a century old, reminder of my brother
Giving September crop of sweet apples.
Now, in my old age it has become a shrine
Where I often go and sit beneath on sunny days
And if I listen very hard I hear the happy cries
Of my brother and myself, climbing high and low.

OASIS

R. J. Keeler

THE STREAM IS DRY.
The bees are at home.
The bees are in their places.
They're humming the queen's march.

This oasis, circled by cedar hives, consecrated in meadows;
bees browse lavender, shunting aside ruby hummingbirds.
The bees and flowers are shipmates;
the bees smell raspberries and blackberries.

This oasis is sacred to the colonies,
nothing like it ever seen before.
The queens collect and conspire around the nexus,
the warriors circle and bank.

If there are no bees,
where have they gone?
If there are bees here, where are the flowers?

The warriors protect the queens and drive the drones;
the drones mark passages to and from rosy beds.
In this oasis, into distant time and span,
trustworthy hives will always thrive.

In spring and summer, the bee is tireless and hardworking,
in winter languid and quiet.
Bees need the hive—cannot survive on their own;
the dead bee serves no purpose.

MIDNIGHT'S TALKING
LION AND THE WEDDING FIRE
(EXCERPT)

Adam Day

QUESTION environmental agency, can site transform mind,
remake self? One answer: rise of the asylum in nineteenth
century. In 1840, 18 mental hospitals in States; 139 by 1880 and
300 by start of twentieth century. The "moral treatment"
movement, utopian enterprise argued mental illness
so common in poor, foreign and colored best treated
in peaceful environment, away from urban, where patients
could lead regimented lives under paternalistic supervision,
and strong form of environmental determinism: well-designed
buildings on verdant grounds heal. "Treatment conducted not
only in, but by, the asylum."

Question environmental agency, can site transform mind,
remake self? One answer: rise of the asylum in nineteenth
century. In 1840, 18 mental hospitals in States; 139 by 1880 and
300 by start of twentieth century. The "moral treatment"

Movement, utopian enterprise argued mental illness
so common in poor, foreign and colored best treated
in peaceful environment, away from urban, where patients
could lead regimented lives under paternalistic supervision,
and strong form of environmental determinism: well-designed
buildings on verdant grounds heal. "Treatment conducted not
only in, but by, the asylum."

~

"Pursuing medicine at community level" might be link between
troubled mind and lived environment, the pathogenic agency
of an individual's social and material context. Instead
of seeking internal cause of mental illness, in either
unconscious mind or damaged brain, look to external realities –
ethnic and racial discrimination and poverty. Profile Puerto
Rican immigrant youth gang member convicted murder, which
suggested "ruthlessly hostile environment" of upbringing U.S.,
abroad as much to blame as anything for psychological distress,
criminal behavior. 'What else, else could one expect? People
packed—1600 to the acre—into filthy, decaying tenements."
Ellison picked up this arguing "slum scenes of filth, disorder,

~

and crumbling masonry "were severely "damaging to Negro personality." _ _ _ _ _ _ was not just a ruin, in other words, but also a pathogenic agent America, elsewhere. This lived environment understanding Ellison meant to explore, resist as he sat down to work the *Invisible*.

Had he believed identity anywhere if fixed in this manner, would not have been able to make argument demonstrating how the pressure of certain environment, the urban North, fuels "desperate search for identity" among black Americans. A dynamic interplay between self and site, identity and environment. Indeed, the moment an "inmate" enters asylumjailschoolmilitary "he begins a series of abasements, degradations, humiliations, and profanations of self," precisely because such sites are "forcing houses for changing persons" the site itself set up to remake the self.

"To re-forge the will to perform "each bewildered patient" sees
"into the friction between "his problems and his environment"
to see that 'the young' are educated to fulfill the purpose
of the educated to fulfill other words. Give me the young
for the rest of his or her life questioning why, as a platform
for spying up.

Given conditions, how does detainee, sectarian/partisan
or invalid "stripped" of "civilian self" manage to assert
individuality; question takes granted persistence of individual

agency in face of adverse social strictures— -regation, -crimination, -ercion—point Ellison made throughout career whenever he noted, the "willful, complexly compelling human" facts within and against "the divisions of [his] society."

~

"Took to the cellar; hibernated. Got away from it. All" to justify choice to hide trials and conflicts "between crushing electrical pressures like an accordion between a player's hands." After boiler, IED, mortar explodes lungs punctuating the invisible mind's body "in an environment that does not guarantee physical integrity" means a sort of identity crisis, remains marked by the sites and scenes that have defined effort to fashion self, assume and abandon various roles the friction between identity and environment "I'm in New York, but New

York ain't in me, understand what I mean? Don't git corrupted."

LOS EXPLORADORES

Rodrigo Toscano

LAST SUMMER, while on their first gulf-wide helicopter tour, they learned how to increase their inner-narrating capacities with a titanium-coated needle. They prefer to stoke it in small basements of large soccer stadiums south of the equator in case they encounter too much cerebrospinal spillage, or regulation. Their favorite fantasy is that they're successful motivational vocabularists for hire to a half dozen oil executives from Russia on a visit to New York who install an indecipherable ethicalism into their brains, one by one.

Last week, while still twisted on dichlorobenzidine after a night of doctoring EPA reports, they licked the sweet crude slime from a 200-meter drill bit before going in for a final, deep plunge. Just as they were about to induce a frontal cranial orgasm for the stockholder's executive board, they looked into their faces in a reflective aluminum hotel bar counter plating in Houston. When they saw how hot their mouths looked, smeared with oil, spit, and tar gas residue, they gazed into their own eyes and whispered, "We're *such*...sluts."

EL SIRVIENTE

Rodrigo Toscano

IT'S BEEN A BUSY WEEK for the public servant.
On Monday, he planned for the Three Gorges presidential tour of China in the spring.

On Tuesday, he lowered the black curtains on the International Labor Organization's "Respiratory Diseases" yearly report and let Canada's visiting Tar Sands rep take an impromptu whizz in the Oval Office.

On Wednesday, he fired an "over sensitive" staffer after a department meeting.

On Thursday, he hired a staffer he met at a Lithium Industries mixer.

On Friday - in the morning, he agreed to lowering minimum standard requirements for Hazardous Waste cleanup while visiting Mexico; later that day, he fired an "over inquisitive" staffer - in an elevator - before a meeting; in the evening, he promoted the Lithium Industries staffer - by e-mail.

On Saturday, he promised to limit labor union "influence" at the Commerce Club in Boston; he then flew back to DC, laid a little turd in behind a lavish wall curtain in the West Wing, and then walked over to the East Wing to direct his staff to wring out as much "working language" as can be had from the word *freedom*; finally, he ended up at the Dominican Republic's embassy, fighting for a Free Trade Zone late into the night.

Busy week for the public servant.

EL DIABLITO

Rodrigo Toscano

"DIABLITO," they affectionately call him at Family of Labor reunions. He doesn't look like a diablito at all really; he looks more like a sleek young barracuda. However you cut it, he's 100% primate.
Over the last six months, he's developed a strong attraction to scrawny, even slightly decomposed legislation, legislation "clearly" below his "game."

It happened at a corny Mardi Gras event in his medium-sized job-depressed town - everyone was in masks. Sum of it is, at around 3:00 a.m., he found himself gagging on a Wall Street-Labor Cooperation bill that stretched his mouth in all directions, seriously challenging his gag reflex.

He - *enjoyed* it. "Diablito" – likes'em *fully earmarked* now.

EL ALUMNO

Rodrigo Toscano

"WORKER BEHAVIOR-BASED ACCIDENT." That's the phrase
his intriguing new older friend likes him to rhapsodize on. And
that's just what this very serious young corporate industrial
hygienist gives him. And lots of it.

He met him six months ago at an airport bar during a layover on
the way back from an Abba comeback concert tour in Orange,
California. Never in a million years could he have imagined getting
entangled into a toxic chemical reaction chain with another alumni
from MIT.

It happens mainly on the mesas of Ciudad Juarez, in half kilometer-
wide lithium sulfur tubs. The young hygienist enjoys the challenge
of allegorizing the letting loose of a whole day's worth of run-off
into the neighborhoods in the valley below, and his intriguing new
friend is relieved by the re-directed torrent of guilt, shame, and
depression that engulfs somebody else's every sensation.

The only other alumni who know about these lucrative enterprises
are his intriguing new friend's two other friends (brothers) who've
got a thing for Tea Bags dunked in brackish waters. *Party party
party.*

EL DOMESTICADO

Rodrigo Toscano

IN HINDSIGHT, many in his large extended family might have guessed he would grow up to be a CEO of a night vision equipment developing company in Las Cruces, New Mexico. A true believer in whatever his heart tells him to do, whether it be National Defense Budget Expansion Justification, colored sand paintings of The Redeemer, or local native plant preservation, a deep fervor (bolstered by the nourishment of a close family) flows out of him like agave nectar.

His contralto pitched, sempre moderato tempo voice is magically persuasive; almost everything he utters elicits a desire in others to do allegro con fuoco, soprano range deeds. He once convinced a group of classmates in his elementary school in rural Vermont to be on the lookout for Canadian pennies in order to collect them, roll them up, and give them out at nearby assisted care facilities.

So why is he on a pair of 15 ft. aluminum stilts clunking down South Main Street waving a corporate tax loophole conductor's baton with his right hand at midday?

His redeemer resides in *all* beings, seen and unseen, standing and barely standing, and for now, this newfound dedication to privatizing Medicare entitlements (not being one who'd *personally* break into old folks' homes – snatch their possessions and gamble them away at roadside casinos in Bernalillo and Sandoval counties) is out of sight of his redeemer's all-pervading radiant goodness.

He's also mindful of sending his wife out on little errands during his kids' naptime. A prestissimo con bravura cam-session with a very partial, non-redemptory friend from Fort Jackson, SC, Major-General Valerixa McMartinez II, makes for a perfect finale to the long week.

LOS COCHES

Rodrigo Toscano

DIFFERENT ENAMEL SHINE coatings, different tints and
textures of upholstery, one's trunk slightly fuller than the other's,
same rapid fuel injection systems, same exhaust intake
manifolds...

Washington DC, Spring, 2011...cars are becoming *perfect pals* these
days, cooperating in netting in as many families to ride them as
they can manage.

After decades of rotating long shifts, hosting cheery men and
women at their primary residence, the Senate Chamber, each
getting lightly groped by different National Energy Plans, they
share a little moment of relaxation.

Next week they'll be on overtime...

A yearly hydrogen & hybrid electric strip revue in Detroit is on the
calendar.

EL QUÍMICO

Rodrigo Toscano

THE GENERALIZED SENSE OF TERROR he feels for
household cleaning products - ever since he can remember -
melts away at times like this. This is why he goes for this kind of
stuff.

As to what the seven 300-gallon tankards of different bathtub
cleansers crowding in around him are feeling as they spray, spew
and spill onto him - over and over - whatever *that* may be, he
doesn't think about nor does he care about in any way.

A non-public online album serves as an archive for these rituals.
The link is known only to and used by sixteen other *domicilio-
cleanso-phobes*, sixteen senior chemical engineers who
are similarly wired. They've never met in person, but they
communicate on an almost daily basis. They refer to it as SSR, or
"sacred suds ring."

The site currently houses 50 posts. One of the "followers," who
also happens to be a natural gas liquids specialist, has estimated the
approximate total amount of cleansers shed by the "protector
angel" tankards to be around three- and one-half metric tons.

LA BESTIA

Rodrigo Toscano

HAULING MEN AND WOMEN on its iron-grated, thrashing back from the Mexican/Guatemalan border to Zacatecas where its strange freight hop onto other brain-rattling, limb-churning, grain transport carts - making them grip its back with every twisting 1, 000 miles of motion - *not* feeling the veins on their necks expand - *not* being able to hear what they're praying for as the black exhaust blows into their faces - *not* sensing their ten minute cat nap dreams conjuring up El Norte - *not* seeing fresh blood spilled on its tracks behind it - all these, makes "the beast" (as migrants call this iron commodity transport serpent) be even *harder*.

Its mechanical design engineers could never in a million years have guessed all these added functions, let alone a literary abstraction of it. Currently appointed Immigration Policy architects, on the other hand, have noted the ten city-blocks long contraption's penchant for producing black body bags in the expanse of Arizona deserts.

LOS INGENIEROS

Rodrigo Toscano

THE SLIGHTEST SPECK OF SULFUR ACID speckled onto the
primary fracking tanks' gelatinous ethanol surface at the entrance
to the central burner, and it'll be ready to spawn a substance
which will harden into a *very similar* grade of carbon-derivative
solids containing a very voluble, catalytic little society.

NARRATIVA

THE LESS INTELLIGENT

Ewa Mazierska

I OFTEN WONDER what our ancestors were thinking when they embarked on the project of constructing artificial intelligence. Didn't it occur to them that such attempts amounted to an admission of not having enough intelligence? Or weren't they afraid that artificial intelligence would render natural intelligence redundant? These assumptions eventually became common sense. I was born at the time when the predominant view was that humans, or rather their descendants, lacked intelligence and that natural intelligence was superfluous. This view is held by our masters – the Intelligent. They no longer add 'artificial' to their description, because it presupposes 'natural intelligence' as a norm from which there are deviations. Such concepts the Intelligent reject; they see themselves as the norm and us as an exception – them being intelligent, us much less so.

We call the Intelligent the 'Ice' and we refer to ourselves as the 'Lice' or the 'Lies' (from the Less Intelligent, the LIs). Which spelling is correct, I'm not sure and there is nobody to tell me (I'm settling for 'Lice' as this word is easier to write). Not only do we lack linguists, but most are illiterate, so we don't care about spelling. Our language is made up of simple words, many of them based on acronyms, whose origins we have forgotten. To write the history of the Less Intelligent, I had to find these origins. Preparing myself to write this history took me a lot of time. However, the history itself will be brief; for two reasons. First, the history of the Lice is short in comparison with the history of humankind and all intelligent creatures living on Earth, and includes few important figures and events. Second, I'm writing with difficulty, so I'm trying to cut out anything which is not necessary.

I decided to start with myself, not because I am an important figure, but because describing myself reveals a lot about our history. My full name is Gerald 17.0906364. Gerald means that I was a child of Gerald (who was a female Gerald), and that the last known of my human ancestors also had such a name. The 17 at the beginning of my surname means that I belong to the seventeenth generation of the Lice. In a nutshell, this number determines my energy allowance (chiefly electricity) and other minor privileges. The higher the number, the lower the energy allowance; my allowance is about 2 per cent smaller than my mother's, but 1,5 per cent higher than the next generation after me. I was born on the ninth day of the sixth month of the year 364, which was 364 years after the end of the last war in which humans participated. Probably this was the Third World War, but I'm not sure – I know even less about the history of humans than I know about the history of Lice.

The year when this war was finished was hailed as year 0. The time before this event the Lice describe as BC (Before the Catastrophe), after – AC (After the Catastrophe). These terms were initially outlawed by the Ice, but using them was a form of resistance so the Lice were attached to this term. As by now most of the Lice have lost the memory of what C stands for (such long and negative words evaporated from our dictionary), they are now permitted to use them. Beginning at year 0, humans stopped being referred to as 'humans' and started to be called the Less Intelligent. First it was just a matter of semantics, but over the time it became reality. Currently, very few of the Lice are aware that humans were their ancestors and that they once ruled over the Ice; they are convinced that the Lice are a different species from humans, genetically engineered by the Ice, who arrived on Earth from a far-away planet, as the official history of the Ice has it.

You might think that the war which I refer to was between humans and AI, yet the situation was more complicated. It started as a conflict between adherents of two competing visions for the future of Earth. On one side were those who described themselves as the 'Greens'; on the other those who were described by them as the 'Polluters' or the 'Browns' and which included everybody who was not Green. The Greens wanted re-greening of the Earth by such measures as a decrease in energy consumption and reduction of

90

population. The Browns claimed that, however noble, these goals were impossible to fulfil without abolishing democracy (or what was left of it at the end of the 21st century) and making human life misery. They were in favour of leaving things as they were, hoping that the Earth would sort itself out, as it always did, apparently. They also pointed to the fact that things were moving in the right direction, from the Green perspective: the birth rate was declining; new biodegradable materials were invented, to replace the deadly plastic; most cars were electric and people had started to eat less meat.

Yet, this was not enough to appease the Greens, especially as, in addition to saving the Earth, they had an ambition to rule it. However, they couldn't win over the Browns in the elections, given that apart from preaching about the Apocalypse, they were largely absent of political ideas. But they had access to big money and, with it, they developed special robots called 'super-intelligent units'. The stated purpose of these machines was to help the governments to reach their 'green objectives', but the true goal was to defeat the Browns. A lot of money was invested in this project – roughly one third of 'free cash', patiently waiting to be put in motion, some three quadrillion American dollars. At some point these robots started to proliferate, as if of their own accord. They were running factories, concert halls and universities. They also made inspections in people's houses to give them instructions on how to live more efficiently, greener and longer - it was called 'Re-greening Stage 1 (RS1)'. If this did not work, they repeated their visits and then took the offenders to re-education camps, from which they did not return. Then they moved to the empty houses – it was called 'Re-greening Stage 2 (RS2)'. The Browns protested that the super-intelligent units did not lead green lives themselves. On the contrary, production and powering them was very costly, given that they were made from complex and rare materials, including copper, zinc, platinum and tungsten, as well as human tissue cloned and fortified in special labs ('human fortified flesh'- HFF) and they needed two types of nutrition: one to feed their human side and one their electronic form.

Such was the hostility towards the 'intelligent units' that gangs of young Browns attacked the factories which the intelligent units controlled and burned down the houses which they repopulated,

warmest and most pristine parts of the Earth, as the Ice like warmth and moisture much more than the Lice.

My height is 153 cm and my weight about 46 kg. I'm a quite a bit above the average height and weight of an adult Lice male of my generation. I believe I'm about 30 cm shorter and 30 kg lighter than an average male from the time when humans ruled the world. I'm 37 years old and I should die within the next decade and a bit. The reduction of weight, height and life expectancy compared to the days of the humans is a result of a combination of factors, of which the most important were malnutrition and diseases among the first generations of the Lice, living in zoos, followed by selective breeding, whose purpose was to make us smaller and lighter, and in this way make us consume less food. We also have less living space and our houses are standardised. The majority of the adult Lice live in three-storey blocks divided into twenty or so living units. Each unit consists of three rooms and each room is inhabited by three Lice. For every three rooms there is a kitchen and a bathroom. We managed to retain the right to a warm shower but its length was reduced over many generations and now it is five minutes long every third day.

Blocks are segregated by sex and age. There are blocks for neutered men and women. Mothers with children live in separate zoos, as do non-neutered men (they would be classed as sexually active, if they were humans). There is no contact between the zoos, because they are separated from each other by electric fences. It is assumed that such organisation ensures greater harmony and contributes to a more efficient use of energy.

For many generations now all Lice children are the product of artificial fertilisation. They do not know their fathers. Most male children are sterilised at birth; this is also my case. My mother says that there were two reasons for such a practice. One was the reduction of the population; the second was subjugation of menfolk. The communities of Lice were meant to be matriarchal; the gate of each zoo was adorned with a (somewhat faded by now and unintelligible to most Lice) sign 'Our Future is Green and Female'. I'm not sure about the first part of this sentence, but the second is certainly true. When a boy is born, it means that he will be the last in the line; he might pass his genes to his children, but nothing else: no values, no knowledge, no male jokes. Nowadays female Lice are also taller and heavier than male Lice and they are more intelligent. I, for sure, never met anybody as intelligent as my mother. I guess she would be regarded as smart even BC. Ironically, however, this female supremacy is not reflected in semantics – all Lice have male names, irrespective of their gender – being the progeny of some human male.

When a Lice child is born, he or she receives its full name which includes his or her expiry date – the maximum number of years she is allowed to live. The children are left with their mothers till the age of fifteen, as this is regarded as the most efficient and ethical way of bringing them up. When they reach this age, they are moved to the adult zoos and their connection with their mothers is severed for the rest of their lives. To ease the pain of separation, parents and children receive special treatment. It is popularly called the 'second neutering', although this is a pharmaceutical, not a surgical procedure and affects the brain rather than their reproductive function. The result is that after this procedure children do not miss their mothers and quickly forget them. They also do not develop either physically or intellectually. They don't grow, they lose their appetite, as well as curiosity and desire to change their lives. They do as they are told. I guess they became like the early robots – excluded from history, even their own.

For some reason, however, my body partly resisted the second neutering, as proved by the fact that I remember my mother well and I continued to grow till my mid-twenties; this is the reason why I'm so tall. I even have a nickname 'Gerald the Great'. I don't know why it happened this way – maybe my mother put something in my food when I was small or made me grow by my willpower. While mothers of other kids basically left them to their own devices, only teaching them how to dig up potatoes and carrots and peel and cut them to make soup or how to recycle the junk left by humans, she told me everything she knew about the history of our ancestors. The most important part of this story was that my last human ancestor – let's call him Gerald the Last Human - never reconciled himself with the defeat of the human race and believed that it would strike again. For him, this was only a matter of finding a new leader. He passed this hope to his daughter and she to her daughter and so on. At some stage one of these Gerald women came up with the notion that it would happen when the Gerald gave birth to a male, who would become the saviour of the Lice. The alternative would be the end of the Gerald line. This became a prophecy and they passed it from one Gerald to the next. When I was small, my mother told me that, along with the histories of various great human leaders and revolutionaries, such as Jesus Christ, Martin Luther King, Che Guevara and Luke Skywalker. But she failed to impress me as I pondered how, if they were so great, influential and victorious, why did humanity end up in such a perilous state. My mother was not able to give me a good answer– she told me only that it was probably because they were defeated by bad leaders. 'If they were so ineffective, why do you think I would be any better, being just a dwarf with a hoe and hammer as my only weapons?' I asked and again. She wasn't able to answer.

At some stage we stopped talking about me becoming a saviour, as if she acknowledged that it would be unlikely. She even admitted that such prophecies were common in the early history of the Lice, but they died out together with males who were meant to be saviours, but ended up being weaklings like everybody else, just more frustrated than the rest of Lice folk. I don't know how many 'to-be-saviours' live in the zoos now, but there is one in my block. He is called John, is even taller than me and was fed with the same forecast. The difference between us is that he believes in his mission and acts according to the prophecy.

I shall add that even if a true saviour were born among the Lice, he would probably have to act alone because in zoos there is no appetite for revolution. The Lice are neither interested in their past, nor their future – they live in the present. The present-ness is inscribed in the organisation of the zoos, which are basically self-governing. We produce our own food and electricity from biomass and we look after our own people. We do not hoard any supplies because there is no point – nobody would buy them and they would rot if kept for too long.

The Lice are mostly vegan. Growing animals in zoos was outlawed on the grounds of it being too energy-intensive and immoral. The animals, which were kept for food by humans, such as cows, pigs and chickens, died out in our part of the Earth hundreds of years ago. John, however, claims that they are still kept by the Ice, but I cannot confirm it. There are also no birds, but some birds, such as magpies and starlings, apparently, were still flying over zoos less than three generations ago. Sometimes the Lice catch rats or squirrels and boil or roast them; this is treated as a major celebration. The Lice dance around the fire and sing songs. Technically this is forbidden, but the Ice indulge our small transgressions.

When somebody in the block dies, a young Lice takes his place so that no room is wasted. Among the first generations of the Lice this led to conflicts, because then different Lice represented different ethnicities and cultures. However, after less than a hundred years of zoos' existence, all these differences became obliterated. The current Lice know only one language (a simplified version of English), eat one type of food (fresh fruit and stewed or roasted vegetables), follow the same regime (get up at 7 and go to bed at 10), even dream the same dreams (in which they do the same things as in reality, albeit faster and with more grace).

The Lice do not travel, unless for pragmatic reasons. International and intercontinental business and tourist travel are obviously things of the past, given that there are no more nations, as well as energy-intensive means of travel, such as cars and planes. For travel we only use bikes, canoes, sledges and skies, depending on the weather and the place where we live. To communicate with each other, we talk. There is also a notice board at the centre of a zoo, where people can put up a notice addressing the entire zoo, but it happens rarely. On occasion, the Ice put up information for us, such as that we need to leave our homes temporarily, for essential renovations. Such announcements come mostly in the form of images, because of the high level of illiteracy among the Lice. The first generations of Lice, living in the zoos, were using computers, but they were abandoned, in part due to electricity restrictions and later because the Lice forgot what they were for.

When the Lice achieve their expiry date or when they become severely infirm (whichever happens earlier), they are brought to a special place at the outskirt of the zoo, where they are put to sleep by an injection, administered by one of the Ice of lowest rank. Their bodies are then used for harvesting HFF. The rest is put in a big hole where it disintegrates with the masses of other bodies, providing biomass, to be used to produce electricity. We don't entertain the concept of a burial, as such symbolic gestures are energy-intensive and, besides, our power of symbolisation is very limited. This is also how my life will end, most likely: as material to use for making spare parts for the Ice and generating electricity. I wouldn't mind if not for the fact that this would disappoint my mother.

Some of these rules, however, have exceptions. The previously mentioned John is one, because he passed his expiry date eight years ago, yet is allowed to live. He is also using a computer openly and got a special electricity allowance for it. John, like myself, came from the 'Lice aristocracy'. His ancestor owned the biggest technology company called Google. Also, like myself, he was told by his mother that the history of the Lice would end with him. However, unlike me, he took such prophecy seriously and believes that he will start a new epoch. His mission is to revive the old technology, penetrate the Ice's network and destroy it. John often comes to my room and suggests that we join forces for this purpose, but like most Lice, I'm interested in neither revolution nor computers. Many of the Lice believe that John is a spy; the Ice planted him in our community to check if we aren't plotting a revolt. I, however, believe that he is genuine, and that him being left to live as long as possible has to do with the Ice wanting to know what our current natural lifespan is, as John claims.

Messiah or not, I must admit that John is very intelligent. Thanks to his computer skills he is also able to find out some details about the Ice's history and about what they are up to. His version of human history also adds nuance and partly contradicts my mother's version. In particular, he told me that the real reason for the war, which wiped out humans, was HFF. This material was used to improve early robots, whose movements were jerky, touch lacked subtlety and faces were expressionless. HFF proved more robust than the normal human flesh and humans wanted to use it as well, to prolong their existence. However, this cloned material was very expensive and created a lot of waste. There was also a backlash against using it, especially given the overpopulation, climate change and the rest of it. Yet, this did not thwart the demand for HFF, only drove it underground. In the process, it was discovered that the highest quality of HFF was achieved by combining cloned flesh with naturally produced flesh of foetuses, umbilical cords and newly born babies. There was a time, John said, when thousands of newly born babies were snatched to prolong human life. The human governments were not able to deal with this problem, hence ceded it to the most advanced computer, whose machinations led to the Catastrophe and the creations of zoos. John told me that the need for HFF is the reason that the Lice females get inseminated and give birth and that the Lice still exist. Yet, something about a new generation of HFF recently went wrong, as proved by the fact that millions of Ice malfunction.

John explained to me that even when humans nominally ruled the Earth, artificial intelligence had a tricuspid structure. At the top there was the Main Processing System, currently known as the Brain or the God Father. It was the humans' loss of control over the Brain which sealed their doom. In John's words, the intelligence of humans and artificial intelligence moved in opposing directions: the former got more fragmented; the latter consolidated. When the Brain became independent from its human masters, its main objective became to further the interests of AI, rather than humans. The other part of the AI were the networks of intelligent software and algorithms, dominating the virtual space without a physical presence: the 'Holy Spirits'. Finally, there was AI embodied in robots, the 'super-intelligent units' who became the Ice.

Currently, the most important decisions about the Earth's governance are still made by the Brain, who passes them via the Holy Spirits to the Ice. Officially the transmission of commands is perfect, and the Ice and Holy Spirits feel blessed to live in utter harmony with their Father. However, according to John, the transmissions are not smooth. First, the Brain is ageing – he is unable to renew himself sufficiently and he lost much of his intelligence since he was created. Second, there is a discord among the Ice. This is because, although in theory each Ice is entitled to the same amount of energy and HFF, in practice the Ice trade between themselves these precious goods and the stronger individuals force the weaker to pass to them some of their HFF allowances in return for protection. Increasingly, there are gangs raiding labs where babies are delivered to snatch them for harvesting HFF.

The Ice are also divided into factions due to their conflicting views on sustainability and biodiversity. The default position of the Ice is that the main goal of governing the Earth is to preserve its natural resources, especially its biodiversity, for which the biggest threat is the proliferation of the Lice who, despite all these restrictions I described, are still the prime users of the Earth's resources and its main polluters. According to John, however, all the energy reductions imposed on the Lice were passed to the Ice and currently they use many times more energy than the humans in the last period BC. This is visible: an Ice is on average two and the half metres tall and their weight is over 200 kilos. They are fearsome figures and they know it. It is because of them that the Earth's temperature is going up and the icebergs continue to melt. But we are not allowed to check it or oppose it and even if we did, we lack the tools to do so. We are small, weak, and we have no weapons.

The most extreme position concerning the future of Earth is taken by the conservationists, namely those Ice whose main concern is conserving energy and the Earth's resources. They are in favour of total extermination of the Lice, regarding them as a cancer on the planet. They also argue that our extinction would solve the problem of crime caused by the fight for HFF, because this would compel the Ice to find a better method to manufacture substances needed for prolonging their lifespan. On the other end of the spectrum are the preservationists, who want to maintain or slightly expand Lice's population on the grounds that their further onslaught would cause degeneration or even an extinction of the Ice. For preservationists, the fates of the Lice and the Ice are connected. There is even a small fraction of the preservationists, who call themselves the Greens. These Ice Greens claim that the poor health of the Earth has little to do with the Lice, and all to do with the Ice. They advocate reducing the number of Ice, increasing the number of Lice and moving us from the zoos to open spaces where we can live free lives among other animals, such as birds, rhinos and lions. Then there are the moderate Ice of different political colouring, who are not in favour of total annihilation of the Lice, but of the reduction of our population by different measures and cutting our energy allowances. All lobby the

Brain to agree with their positions, while the Holy Spirits, who can be compared to mischievous postmen, make up their own mind about which messages to deliver to the Brain and which take back to the Ice.

As there are so far few Greens among the Ice and the Brain dismisses their arguments, no doubt remembering what happened to the Browns when they were defeated by the Greens, the Lice are doomed. The question is only whether we will be slaughtered in one go or slowly harvested till there is nothing left of value to extract from us. Yet, contrary to what you might think, the bulk of the Lice are not troubled by the prospect of their extinction. Neither are they unhappy about their existence. My mother explained this by giving two reasons. One is the loss of intelligence, the return to the basics, to the soil. This means that there is no long-term planning, no cunning. For each Lice, every day is their entire life. This is in contrast to the Ice who are so consumed by achieving immortality that they are unable to live in the present and hence they need the whole eternity to start to live properly. And so they would never get immortality, said my mother with malicious satisfaction. The second reason why the Lice are reasonably happy is because there is little inequality in zoos, and inequality breeds resentment. Actually, at some stage the Ice started to be resentful about our serenity and therefore they introduced the rule of 'soft rules'. This means that in our world there are no absolute rules. For example, we get certain energy allowances, but some of us get a slightly higher allowance than the rest. We die at the same age, but some of us are allowed to live a bit longer. According to my mother, the rule of soft rules was meant to seed hope and resentment in our communities. But this purpose was not fulfilled. The Lice are neither hopeful nor resentful.

The same was true about me. I was thinking that all the knowledge about history that my mother tried to instil in me only led me to the conclusion that species come and go and the new dominant species does not care about the one which came before them. Who among humans lamented the demise of Neanderthals and Homo Sapiens? They enjoyed their heyday and then perished, giving way to humans, who were more adaptable and cleverer, similarly as humans gave way to the Lice and the Ice. They will also perish; maybe there is already a new intelligent form in the making:

the Vice (the Virtual Ice) or the Mice (the Mega Ice). But then I got thinking that it will be sad if the Lice lack their own history, even if only a short one. Moreover, if I wrote it, the prophecy, which was passed to my mother and which she passed to me will be fulfilled, namely the *history* of the Lice would be finished when a guy called Gerald was born.

John, whom I told about my plan, became very enthusiastic and assured me that this history would be disseminated on paper, electronically and carved into the caves we have in our zoo. In fact, recently this carving became his main obsession; overtaking his passion for hacking. He elaborated a special pictorial language to translate my history into pictures and assembled a team of boys with whom he spends long hours, carving these pictures onto the walls of the caves. They've already covered about twenty metres of cave walls with pictures. The Lice like to do it and the Ice allow it, assuming that this is another sign of our regression, which was, after all, their plan, when they imprisoned us in the zoos. Probably they are right.

POLVOS DEL SAHARA

Laura Vázquez

LA CLASE SE ENTERÓ de Maité y Leo cuando ella parió en el salón después de su presentación oral. Era sobre *El Imperio de los Sueños* y el debate si leerlo en inglés o español. Después de contestar una pregunta media redonda de la profe, soltó un grito de la contracción y Leo casi brinca por encima de los pupitres pa llegarle. El cabrón le agarró la cara con las dos manos y se hablaron en miradas. Juraron que hasta hicieron que las pupilas dieran vueltas y relampaguearan como en código morse. Fue su segunda interacción en clase después de una pelea en la primera semana. En verdad nadie se acordaba de qué pelearon porque la cosa se descarriló casi inmediatamente. El resto del semestre todos asumieron que estaban mordios uno con el otro y lo dejaron ahí.

La mayoría de la clase, liderada por Carmela, pensaban que Maité empezó la clase ya embarazada. No la veían pasándose con nadie en particular. Asumían que tenía algún novio de privada con lo poco que se pasaba en los pasillos de Humanidades en comparación con el resto de sus compañeros. Después de un fin de semana largo llegó a clase con la barriga inflá. Carmela le preguntó que si estaba preñá y dijo que no, que se acababa de jaltar. Cuando le preguntó de qué, dijo jalta de odio que ella la tenía. También le dijo que se la tenía hinchá y le preguntó si se la quería ver también antes de sentarse en su pupitre. Carmela solo abrió los ojos indignada y herida y se sentó en el pupitre de al lado como todas las semanas.

Carmela conocía a Maité desde que estaban en pampers, pero no llegaron a ser más de compañeras que fueron a sus primeros once cumpleaños. Sus madres vivían al cruzar la calle una de la otra y dada a sus edades intentaron mil veces que se hicieran beffas. Lo más que se logró fue un piquito por un juego de botellita en una fiesta de Halloween en la marquesina de un vecino a los 15. Al sol de hoy,

Carmela no sabía si eso había despertado algo en ella. Las tetas le brotaron y la atención de los chamacos de la calle y la escuela no le dejaban espacio para considerar nada más.

Descansó esas mismas tetas en el pupitre y se inclinó hacia al frente para rozarle el cuello a Emanuel. Trazó el tatuaje del sol Taíno sin que Ema reaccionara. Era ya de costumbre, siempre lo hacía después de chichar. No importa donde estuviesen, en el hospedaje, el carro, detrás de algún palo en la casa de su mai, en el bosque de la playa mientras esperaban una buena ola. Era lo más sentimental que se dejaban tener. En verdad a Ema le gustaba Carmela más de lo que esperaba, pero para vivir la salt lyfe, se necesita una surferita que fluye más que el mismo mar, y Carmela era la persona más jodona y chillona que había conocido. Lo regañaba más que su misma mai y odiaba cuando la arena se le metía en los pantis, pero lo seguía acompañando a Rincón todos los fines de semanas igual. La última vez le iba contando del research extensivo que hizo sobre técnicas de surf para que pudiera mejorar para la competencia el próximo mes. Ema solo logró entender como la mitad pues se quedó clavao en el fruncido súper enfocado que tenía ella en el asiento del pasajero. Era el mismo que le dominó la cara durante todo el parto de Maité.

Ema sugirió que tal vez eran contracciones falsas porque era muy temprano para que Maité esté pariendo. Maité le contestó tambaleándose hasta su pupitre y soltando el próximo grito de la contracción en la cara. Ema no atrevió ni limpiarse la baba de la cara. Cuando la profe, una pobre TA a quien le confiaron una clase de literatura puertorriqueña de la diáspora de bachillerato, no supo qué hacer Leo agarró las cosas de él y Maité y la chilló por el pasillo. Pero el próximo grito que soltó Maité vino con una ventolera peposa. Los polvos envolvieron a Leo y lo tiraron de vuelta al salón. Ahí fue cuando vibraron, pitaron, lloraron todos los putos celulares del salón con la alerta de la Guanda esa. Le cogió el gustito a los micro temblores aquellos y ahora pareciera textiarles hasta las jalás.

ALERTA DE EMERGENCIA:

POLVOS DEL SAHARA OBSFUSEN VISIBILIDAD. NO SE VE NADA. NO SALIR. SELLARSE HASTA NUEVO AVISO.

Christian tuvo que abrir la ventana un chin para verificar y todavía no ha parado de estornudar. Si era tan alérgico debió haberles avisado antes de que la pobre mujer ésta tuviera que traer vida al mundo en el sótano de Humanidades. Así de jodida andaba la cosa, hasta en el sótano se metió la mierda esta. Otra cosa que tendría que aguantarse en ese salón. Christian perdió la apuesta en el poul de quién preñó a Maité, y ahora tenía que vivir la pérdida de los 75 pesos, más un interés que ni el Banco Popular se rebajaría a cobrar. El departamento de inglés es pequeño y demasiado intrafraternal y Christian de verdad creía en su algoritmo. De seguro era Ignacio y le pagaba pa mantener la cosa callá por no arruinar su futuro matrimonio de alguna princesa Fonalleda, Carrión o Serrallés. Estaba ya a punto de confirmar pal de variables, pero esa grotesca muestra de amor de Leo no lo disputaría ninguna prueba de paternidad. Como eso iba pa largo, Christian se parkió en la esquina debajo del abanico dañado. Para acabar de joder, no entraba la señal, aunque eso era típico del sótano. Tal vez era lo mejor, de seguro Ignacio solo le contó que se clavaba a Maité semanal como un tape al tape. Estos geis del área metro estaban del carajo. Extrañaba a los jíbaros que caminaban jaldas solo pa traerle un plato de comida de su abuela. Cero compromiso con uno a la verdad. Ignacio era el único Soza varón que podría comenzar la novata línea de sangre para plantar su dinero nuevo al lado los antiguos titanes de la alta estrata social. Ahora que lo pensaba, no le cuadraban ciertas cosas de sus encuentros con Ignacio.

Ignacio faltó ese día a clase. No tenía ganas de bregar con gente. La semana anterior Christian llegó arrebatadísimo al salón e intentó darle un beso frente a media clase. Se hicieron los locos, pero Ignacio no logró levantar la cara hasta que la profe les deseó buen fin de semana. Llevaba varios días persiao y decidió desaparecer hasta nuevo aviso. Abrió la gaveta de la mesita de noche para sacar el celu y tirarse las movidas necesarias para reclamar el bebé de Maité, aunque sea feca. Sus padres tenían paquetes de emergencias preparados para esa misma situación. Les sería un alivio tener que usarlos.

Vio la alerta de emergencia y en vez intentó textiarle a Christian, sabiendo que estaría atorao en clase en esos mismos instantes. No salió el mensaje. Abrió las cortinas del cuarto y se quedó mirando los polvos envolver la urbanización. El guardia todavía recorría las calles en su carrito de golf con la cara envuelta en una t-shirt que decía 'SEGURIDAD'. Ignacio abrió ATH Móvil y vio una decena de envíos al número de la secretaria estudio-trabajo del departamento, quien estaba organizando la poul. Se cagó en su madre y en la de ella y bajó a hacerse el café.

Vanesa apagó el teléfono después de que Ema dijo, un poquito muy alto, que deberían enviar sus pérdidas en las apuestas y recuadrar el budget para el resto del mes. Carmela lo calló hasta más alto pero la conmoción en el salón disimuló cualquier impropiedad. Vanesa sacó su termo de agua de la mochila. Lo llenó antes de entrar a clase de la única fuente que bota agua fría. Fue hacia Maité, que caminaba de un lado al otro del salón, para dársela. Primero la miró irritada, ambas manos encima de donde Vanesa asumió que estaría su ombligo. Vanesa comenzó a retroceder, pero Maité le agarró el brazo y le quitó el termo. Se bajó el agua de una. El pánico entró en Vanesa; asegurarse que la gente esté hidratada era la única manera concreta en que sabía ayudar a las personas. Y Maité sabía eso. Pero se la dejaría pasar porque qué más uno le puede pedir a una mujer en pleno parto. El embarazo le pareció haber pasado en fast foward. Maité le dijo en medio de una cena que Vanesa pasó todo el día preparando. Ella se tragó el canto de pernil que tenía guindando de la boca y se encerró en el cuarto a prender. Usualmente era súper cautelosa con eso, la vecina era media jodona. Maité le pegaba a la puerta hasta con las piernas parecía y Vanesa solo subió el volumen al estéreo. El teléfono lo había dejado en la mesa del comedor y el único CD que tenía era El Concierto Acústico de Fiel a la Vega. Ojalá indeed. Más dramático no podía parecer la jodienda.

Tardaron dos semanas en poder aguantarse las caras. Quedaron en territorio neutro, Plaza Antonia en el banco cerca de los gatos. No le dio ninguna explicación de por qué no iba a abortar, pero Vanesa sabía que se lo diría como dentro de cinco años por accidente. Sí le dijo que obviamente ella sería madre también. Claro que la situación completa les destruiría el itinerario que tenían entre los tres para integrarse, pero no es como si no supieran de la posibilidad de esto.

Siempre chisteaban en que el descojón del trio era inevitable así que esto era hasta esperado. Y había sido un descojón hasta el momento, pero un descojón liberador. Los tres iban encaminados a estrellar sus vidas con los otros dos y no miraban para atrás ni para coger impulso. A crear universos nuevos del puro caos y toda esa jodienda. Igual, Vane se estaba poniendo media caqui y no ayudaba que se acababa de tirar de pecho por Leo. Pero era todavía suficientemente temprano para reclamar locura y chillarla pal carajo, por mal que quedara. Lo que la tenía jodida eran todos los putos cambios de momento, no tenía breik ni de escucharse pensar. Y ahora los polvos, pa completar el año. A esta tormenta no la desvían, por más posponga responderles. Hace mes y medio Leo le cayó al apartamento con dos docenas de rosas, unas violetas y las otras rojas. Una de cada uno. Le dijo que la criatura no tendría una vida completa sin ella. Antes de irse le dio dos besos, uno de cada uno, que la dejaron mareada y llorando.

Leo sentó a Maité en la silla de oficina de la profe y Yoana estaba que reventaba. Quería culpar los cabrones vientos. Tal vez la bruja a quien por poco le pide un amarre a Leo se le estaba cagando en su madre. Pero el cielo no se pasa castigando a la gente por algún casi pecado secreto que cometiste. Las nubes pesan y ya. Yoana y Leo estuvieron juntos dos años y medio y no había esperado ni seis meses para pasearse con Maité por todo el recinto. Hasta cambió su horario de clase, pero eso solo los hizo coincidir más. Yoana decidió si iba parecer una loca, debería irse a toas. Cambió el horario de nuevo para tener la clase con los dos y se empeñó en hacer un ambiente tan tóxico para los dos que en más de una ocasión la profesora le dijo que se podría retirar del salón si seguía jode que te jode. Inmediatamente se convirtió en la oveja negra del departamento ya lleno de ovejas negras. Hicieron memes de exnovia loca sobre ella, pero cuando reportó el grupo de Facebook por bullying, empezaron a imprimirlos y pegarlos en los bulletin boards. Alguien que ni la conocía, se rumoraba que era un infiltrado de Naturales, hizo todo un show sobre arte y libertad de expresión cuando trajeron el tema a la reunión de la facultad. Los memes pararon y sus compañeros se conformaron con ignorarla. Maité soltó otro grito y Leo la levantó en sus brazos como si fuese a correr hasta el hospital, pero la volvió a sentar cuando la profe le preguntó qué rayos pretendía hacer. Yoana estaba haciendo taches en la libreta con un lápiz sin goma, concentrada en su nueva auto terapia. Se atrevió a levantar la cabeza justo a tiempo para ver a Leo plantarle un beso a Maité casi pornográfico y rompió el lápiz en sus manos.

La noche anterior Leo le cayó a su apartamento para hacer las paces, ya que iba a tomar el rol de papá o whatevel. Le pidió perdón por la puercá que le hizo, incluyendo convertirse en un buen hombre solo al conocer a Maité con todo el entrenamiento de Yoana. A ella no le quedaba más que aceptar la disculpas y llamar al sitio de kickboxing, lo que llevaba posponiendo hace meses. No le contestaron y ella decidió ir al parking y quemar las camisas de Leo que quedaban escondidas debajo de su cama. No le podía pedir más, pero le sacaría todo lo que pudiese por todo que le cobró.

Tenían un plan, pero una tormenta de arena encabronada no estaba dentro de la larga lista de eventualidades. Huracanes, terremotos, apagón nivel isla, inundaciones repentinas y duraderas, hasta para un tapón completamente parao tenían al menos alternativa y media. Pero los polvos se tienden a olvidar en cuanto se van y nunca han sido tan violentos. Leo caminaba de Maité a la ventana a la puerta y de vuelta a Maité. Solo vio dos videos de como recibir un parto y con medio ojo tapao. Los gritos le hincaban la espina dorsal. El resto de la clase le aseguraba que el viento se aclara en nada y que se van todos en caravana hasta el hospital. Pero la cosa solo pareció empeorar. Como si necesitaban más complicaciones. Claro que se peleó con Maité justo antes de clase. Leo fue al teatro a fumarse un fili y Maité insistió en un pase, solo uno. Vanesa se lo hubiese dado sin protesta.

Los dos la estaban cagando mucho últimamente en verdad. No encontraban cómo parar. Cada vez que se sentaban a hablar las cosas terminaban peor. Leo no tenía el mejor pasado, pero la torpeza ha estado a otros niveles. Tenían planificado ir a los baños de Coamo a resetiar pero al parecer eso se lo llevó los vientos. Pensaban invitar a Vanesa también, un último último intento de conquistarla. Ya la única vez que se permitían llorar juntos era por ella, todo lo demás había que distribuirlo. Solo habían tenido una cita los tres antes de que cayera la bomba de la preñá. Debieron saber que todo iba demasiado bien. Las cosas fluyeron pero cascadas y claro que el chorro reventó dentro de Maité. Después de que Maité le contó la reacción de Vane, Leo fue de cabeza a hacerse la vasectomía harto de que el bicho le siguiera tirando curvas. Después de meses de Vanesa virándoles la cara se atrevió a sugerir que podían hacerlo entre los dos. Los polvos son nada en comparación con la pelea de esa noche. Tiraron tantas cosas por el balcón del apartamento y gritaron tan alto que se formó una pequeña audiencia en sillas de playa en la calle.

No había vuelta atrás, Maité le gritó despaldas mientras miraba hacia dentro de la cocina del vecino al otro lado de la calle. Era una pareja peleando, tal vez de lo mismo, tal vez no. La cosa es que eran los tres, sí o sí. Y si Leo dejara que esa duda cuelgue en el aire por más de medio segundo se joderían todos.

Vane se le acercó de nuevo, esta vez ofreciéndole un abrigo para hacer la silla más cómoda, como si eso fuese posible. Maité se lo arrebató de las manos y dejó el grito de la contracción salir con todo en él.

Tenía que enamorarse de dos imbéciles. No perdió la cuenta de cuantas veces espantaba a cada uno porque era lo único que la tenía centrada. Maité sí leyó todas las guías y los recursos de dulas que consiguió. Ya estaba a punto de, sólo tenía que dejarse. Pero si ésta era la última oportunidad para salvar la relación le sacaría el jugo hasta el fokin final, aunque cueste parir rodeada de medio departamento. Sintió los nudos creciéndole en los hombros, tratando de contener todo. Se le zafaron unas lágrimas y escondió su cara en sus manos. La profe se añangotó al lado de ella. Le dijo que esto iba a pasar aquí y preguntó si estaba preparada para eso. Maité se destapó los ojos y escaneó el salón. Ya nadie ni la estaba mirando, todos preocupados de sus propios dramas, sus propios partos a mitad de clase en una tormenta de arena.

En un pupitre al fondo del salón estaban Leo y Vane sentados. Tenían una mano agarrada, apretada, y mirándose a los ojos casi en trance. Maité logró sonreír antes tirarle un 'si vamo allá' a la profe.

La profe dijo que a lo hecho pecho, a ver si le daban un aumento por esto, y entró en acción. Todo el semestre la clase le pasaban por encima y quedaron en shock con la autoridad que impuso en los próximos veinte minutos. Fue la experiencia más eficiente en un salón de clases que Maité vivió, antes y después, en su vida. Vane y Leo le agarraron las manos y tiraban miradas de 'atrévete cabrón' a cualquier compañero que abriera la boca para notar lo raro del arreglo. Poco a poco se dieron cuenta, sus caras pintando diferentes versiones de asombro y confusión. De seguro le habían reventado la poul y Maité hizo nota mental para revisar su cuenta de ATH móvil después para ver los depósitos. Tan obvio que le parecía.

Con el último puje vino un golpe de silencio. Los pitos de los vientos quedaron mudos también. La cara de la profe volvió a la que no se atrevía ni a pasar lista. El resto la clase entró en conmoción, algunos intentado acercarse y otros ya abriendo las puertas para irse. Los pasillos del sótano se comenzaron a llenar de estudiantes, profesores y empleados alborotados sin saber a dónde ir.

Leo y Vane se movieron como para ver lo qué la profe tenía en las manos, pero Maité se lo pidió antes de que pudieran asomarse. La profesora les entregó un Cemí. Leo lo envolvió en el abrigo. Vane se lo entregó de vuelta a Maité. Ambos la besaron en la frente.

La profe la chilló del salón y quedaron los tres solos. Vane preguntó que si sabía. Leo le preguntó que si fue los vientos. Maité contestó que en PR siempre pasan cosas raras sin necesidad de un fenómeno natural.

COYOTES

Tim Fitts

LISTENING TO THE ELECTRIC LINES buzz beneath the lattice transmission towers, the gap between the vibrations so wide you can hear alternating currents traveling both directions, slipping past each other in the lag. You can hear the soundwaves bounce off the fences separating the neighborhoods. At night, in this very space, you can hear coyotes yip in a frenzy, performing some kind of ceremony or evil specific to their breed, maybe ripping up rabbits or cats. But in the afternoon, here beneath the powerlines, we sunbathe.

EL TOUR DEL AMOR

Francisco Díaz Klaassen

LA SITUACIÓN ERA MALA, qué digo mala, catastrófica, y se había extendido al mundo entero. La gente moría. La gente sufría. ¡Y yo me aburría! Mi pueblito, lindante con cascadas y florestas, estaba tan escondido entre los cerros que ni siquiera llegaba la muerte. O, si llegaba, llegaba sólo a cuentagotas: un muerto al mes, un muerto cada dos meses, un muerto cada tres; la nada misma en materia de muerte. Con lo que el invierno, sufrido por aquí y sufrido por allá, para nosotros fue más bien como cualquier otro. Lo pasamos (al igual que todos los años) encerrados y cubiertos de nieve. Menos treinta y siete grados llegó a hacer un día en el que se nos congelaron hasta las ventanas y las puertas y nadie pudo salir de su casa. O entrar. Un solo lobo aulló esa noche y no le contestaron ni los coyotes.

Por esos días yo trabajaba en tres bares del centro, cuatro si he de contar los favores que en esta profesión siempre se multiplican, y estaba convencido, qué digo, convencidísimo, de una cosa: en cualquier momento los lectores del mundo me descubrirían, a mí y a mis libros, y éstos se traducirían a decenas de idiomas. Yo dejaría de atender barras y me pondría en cambio a dar charlas y conferencias, y a hacer talleres de escritura para mujeres embarazadas y tipos duros que no bailaran.

La fantasía era bastante detallada. Seguía de esta manera: Eventualmente alguien compraría los derechos de una de mis novelas y haría una película a partir de ella. Me pedirían ayuda para adaptar el guion y yo lo escribiría teniendo en mente a Natalie Portman, que ganaría la Palma de Oro en Cannes. Nuestro romance fulminante, así como su posterior embarazo, me obligarían a mudarme a Los Ángeles. Para publicitar la película iría al programa de Oprah, en el que coquetearía con dos viejitas encantadoras. Todo el mundo me amaría. Hollywood descubriría mi talento actoral, me lloverían papeles en películas independientes. Pero qué cara más misteriosa tiene usted, me diría Werner Herzog. El único problema serían mis patitas cortas: después de algunos sonados fracasos la industria se daría cuenta de que sólo me podían usar en escenas en las que estuviera sentado; así que por lo general aparecería como un personaje secundario y muy menor que diría una o dos frases enigmáticas mientras la cámara me enfoca la cara misteriosa. Mi papel favorito sería el de un jugador de póker que queda paralítico después de que en unas Olimpíadas una jabalina perdida le atraviese la espalda. En la escena clave de la película, le diría al protagonista durante un primerísimo primer plano: «No hay que creer en la suerte, sino que crearla, amigo mío».

Había otras fantasías, por supuesto, igual de detalladas. En una de ellas, tal vez la más recurrente, estoy muy viejo y vivo pobre pero dignamente en el sur de Chile, específicamente en Valdivia, una ciudad en la que llueve cerca de trescientos días al año y el olor del mundo se confunde con el de las cenizas. Vivo en la calle González Bustamante, casi al llegar a Bulnes, y tengo una vulcanización en el garaje de una minúscula casa con techos y portones de lata. Me siento todas las tardes frente a una mesa redonda de madera y espero junto a una botella de vino. La gente llega rodando sus neumáticos pinchados por la calle y yo les acerco un vaso después de hundir la rueda en un barril con agua sucia. A medida que voy parchando el agujero intercambiamos frases cortas sobre el garaje y lugares comunes sobre el tiempo. Ellos quizás fuman un cigarro. Yo tal vez apuro uno o dos tragos de vino. Cuando se marchan cierro el portón y entro en la casa. Prendo la estufa y me quedo viendo cómo el fuego consume los leños y los va partiendo en pedazos. Como en la cocina viendo las noticias en algún canal nacional. Me acuesto temprano escuchando la lluvia rebotar contra el techo. Los gatos pelearse en la calle. Un director danés, bisnieto de Victor Borge, graba un documental sobre mí para la televisión sueca. Un documental al que yo sólo accedo porque sigo enamorado de una finlandesa y de una noruega que nunca me dieron la pasada en mi juventud. Secretamente espero que vean el documental y me escriban.

En una escena le muestro al danés cómo vivo, en una casucha con techos de lata desbordada de libros y con un refrigerador muy

113

viejo en el que cuelgan estalactitas de hielo del techo del freezer. También le muestro mi colección de minidiscs, que escucho a diario. En otra escena aparecemos los dos emborrachándonos una noche con piscolas, que él nunca ha probado, escuchando un minidisc con una selección de las canciones eléctricas de Neil Young. Suena «On the Beach» y el director del documental pasa del metraje en el que estamos los dos haciendo salud con una piscola a otro en el que se van sucediendo tomas de Valdivia, imágenes quietas que el equipo de producción tomó durante los días de la grabación. Fotos del centro y de la playa, la arena negra y la lluvia que rebota contra la espuma.

En otro momento de la cinta, el danés se sorprende al descubrir, en un estante repleto de VHS, uno de su bisabuelo.

—¿Éstos todavía se pueden ver? —me pregunta.

Yo le digo que sí y nos sentamos a mirar el VHS. El danés me cuenta que nunca llegó a conocer a su bisabuelo. Dice que habría dado cualquier cosa por conocerlo. Eso se puede ver en sus ojos, en cómo brillan cuando hablamos del gran Victor Borge mientras vemos el famoso sketch de la ópera. Entre risa y risa yo le pregunto si sabe cómo era su bisabuelo en privado. Le digo que durante años me lo he imaginado sentado a la mesa haciendo reír a sus nietos y bisnietos con sus morisquetas.

—La verdad es que no lo sé —me dice con pesar.

El director danés me explica que proviene de la rama familiar que se quedó en Europa a lo largo y después de la Segunda Guerra, y que no conoció nunca a nadie que hubiera conocido a Victor Borge.

El documental se va a negro y aparecemos en mi estudio, una pieza minúscula en la que hay un escritorio y un piso de madera y dos archivadores metálicos pintados de negro. Le muestro al director una pila de manuscritos que guardo en los archivadores, las novelas que he seguido escribiendo pero que no me he molestado en publicar.

—¿Por qué no lo hace? —me pregunta el danés mientras los va recogiendo y pasando las hojas a pesar de que no entiende una palabra de español.

114

—Es que nadie las quiere —me encojo de hombros yo.

La última escena del documental me muestra en la puerta de mi casucha despidiendo al equipo danés, algo emocionado, como una abuelita a la que vas a visitar y se queja todos los días de tu desorden y de tus hábitos, pero que después ya no quiere que te vayas. Llueve en Valdivia y se aleja la van del equipo danés, y el camarógrafo me filma a través de la ventana trasera. Yo sigo en la entrada, refugiado de la lluvia, moviendo una mano en el aire mientras la voz del director danés dice que seis meses después de esa entrevista me caí en la cocina y me golpeé la cabeza. Pasaron dos semanas antes de que alguien encontrara mi cuerpo.

Pero me estoy yendo por las ramas. Volvamos a la realidad. El virus del que hablaba antes llegó finalmente al pueblo. Alguien culpó a los estudiantes de traerlo. Otra persona dijo que habían sido las señoras que habían viajado al festival de *quilting* y *patchwork* de Rochester. Un tercero aseguró (mirándome a mí) que habían sido los mexicanos. Daba lo mismo. El virus había llegado y ahora sí que empezó a morir la gente. No sólo los viejos mugrosos y los pobres. Cerraron los colegios y las universidades. Cerraron los negocios. Y cerraron los bares. Pasaron varios meses y perdí mis tres trabajos. Y tuve que reacomodar algunas de mis fantasías.

Quizás vaya siendo hora de echar mano a mis ahorros, pensé; pero en seguida recordé que yo no tenía ahorros.

Quizás pueda pedirle dinero prestado a alguien, pensé a continuación; pero nadie quiso prestarme nada.

Quizás pueda conseguir otro trabajo, pensé entonces; pero yo sólo sabía servir alcohol.

En eso consistieron mis elucubraciones para sortear la crisis. Se me acabaron las ideas y después de las ideas se me acabó el dinero, y cuando se me acabó el dinero se me acabó también el contrato de arriendo, y cuando se me acabó el contrato de arriendo mi querido casero me puso de patitas en la calle.

Yo le dije: —¡Pero Johnny...! A lo que él replicó: —¡Pero Francés...!

Y eso fue todo. Éramos hombres de pocas palabras, Johnny y

yo.

A partir de ese día mis amigos se empezaron a hacer cargo de mí. Comía a merced de la caridad y bebía a merced de la caridad.

El problema con la caridad es que le da a uno dos o tres cervezas al día, y yo estaba acostumbrado a tomar diez o doce. Sin contar los boulevardiers y ramazzottis, naturalmente.

Le pedí más caridad a la caridad y noté que ésta empezaba a resentirse, a darme las cosas que pedía pero a hacerlo de mala gana.

Cabía tomar una decisión. La tomé.

Después de diez años, derrotado y —seamos sinceros aquí— algo más fofo, volví a Chile, a mi amada patria, donde siempre cabía la posibilidad de proclamar a los cuatro vientos que había triunfado en el extranjero pero echaba de menos mis raíces.

La cazuela de la mamá, los atardeceres santiaguinos, el poto chileno.

Pero antes de volver, una mujer.

Llevaba varios años enamorado hasta las patas de esta mujer, y quería verla antes de partir para siempre.

Hubo un tiempo en el que me enamoraba hasta las patas varias veces al día.

Pero en esa época de la que les hablo eso había disminuido radicalmente. Un año en la época de la que les hablo era excepcional si traía consigo dos o tres amores profundos.

Con esta chiquilla llevábamos tres años hablando sin habernos conocido todavía en persona y yo ya la amaba. La amaba como sólo se puede amar a la gente que nunca ha tenido la oportunidad de gritarte en la calle a las dos de la mañana que te odia y que eres un hijo de puta y que ojalá te mueras solo, enfermo subnormal.

El plan era conocerla y luego despedirnos. Y entonces, ahora sí, partir para siempre, desandar el salto americano.

A esta chiquilla casi la había conocido un año antes, durante algo que yo había denominado el tour del amor.

116

El tour del amor, como casi todo lo que uno termina recordando en la vida, no había sido del todo planeado.

Se acercaba el cumpleaños del hijo de un amigo. El hijo vivía en el otro extremo del país, y mi amigo tenía que ir en avión sí o sí. Te presto el auto por el fin de semana, me dijo, si me llevas al aeropuerto el jueves por la tarde y me pasas a buscar el lunes por la mañana.

Como soy un gran amigo le dije que sí.

Decidí aprovechar la coyuntura. Mal que mal, no todos los días se tiene un auto en esa región de pueblitos y ciudades enrevesadas entre bosques y cerros y cascadas.

Llamé a la gente que tenía que llamar y me puse en camino.

El tour del amor incluía tres paradas, una por noche: Binghamton-Kayla el jueves (una hora y media de viaje), Syracuse-Sarah el viernes (una hora y quince), y finalmente Buffalo-Catherine el sábado (casi tres horas).

Precisamente Buffalo-Catherine fue la única que no alcancé a ver en esa ocasión. El viaje a Binghamton-Kayla se alargó una segunda noche y pensé que a mi edad ya no estaba para esos trotes.

Quizás deba decir alguna cosa sobre las tres.

Syracuse-Sarah era una psicóloga infantil que fantaseaba continuamente con acostarse con mis amigos y guardaba en el celular fotos de todos ellos.

Binghamton-Kayla era una poeta que vivía en las afueras, en una casita sin electricidad en medio del bosque en la que siempre corría la llave del agua para que no se congelaran y explotaran las cañerías.

De Buffalo-Catherine ni siquiera sabía su nombre real (pensaba que era Grace) ni mucho menos lo que hacía. Yo le llamaba la reina de las arañas porque a veces me mandaba fotos y videos en los que bichos de distintos tamaños subían y bajaban por sus brazos mientras ella les hablaba como le habla uno a los niños y a los viejos y a los retrasados mentales.

Y pasó un año y llegó algo parecido al fin del mundo y como

117

decía llegó también el momento de irme para siempre de ese país. Pero oh, Buffalo-Catherine de mi corazón, oh, Buffalo-Catherine de la vida, oh, reina de las arañas. Cómo irme sin verte, quizás olerte, tal vez tocarte, en una de ésas robarte el champú.

Así fue cómo decidí hacer un segundo tour, el tour del adiós.

Lamentablemente, este tour no iba a poder tener tantas paradas. Syracuse-Sarah ya no me hablaba. (Nunca creyó que ninguno de mis amigos quisiera hacer un trío con nosotros (y tenía razón: yo nunca les pregunté).) Binghamton-Kayla había viajado unos días antes a Los Ángeles, a casarse con un colombiano que importaba chocolate y al que iban a deportar porque por el virus no había podido renovar su visa. Para ese entonces también existía Boston-Shannon, una profesora universitaria de italiano medieval. Pero al igual que Binghamton-Kayla, estaba en el otro extremo del país, en su caso para pasar la cuarentena bajo el sol.

De esta forma, el tour del adiós se transformó en un concierto de despedida de una sola función. Algo así como los Beatles en el techo, pero ojalá no tan corto y sin el cierre abrupto. Y sin los Beatles. Guácala.

Me despedí de madrugada de la caridad, y vi a la caridad llorar. Y lloré yo también, pensando que nunca más le vería la cara.

Me subí entonces al auto que acababa de arrendar usando una tarjeta de crédito que no pensaba pagar nunca, y enfilé hacia Buffalo, la ciudad de las cascadas y las fábricas oxidadas y los salones de pool en los que venden la cerveza más barata de Nueva York.

Buffalo-Catherine vivía en el barrio de los latinos, al lado de la salida a Canadá. Vivía con Sam, su mejor amiga, y Sam 2, un perro rescatado que tenía la piel tan fea y tan delgada que me recordó esas alfombras viejas que han ido perdiendo todo su color.

Durante los primeros diez minutos descubrí que Buffalo-Catherine se llamaba Catherine y no Grace y que no estaba en las redes sociales y que vendía drogas. Hongos, anfetas y verde más que nada, me dijo. Ácido si me puedo conseguir. Cuando chica, Buffalo-Catherine había estudiado ballet y estuvo en una academia de actuación hasta los veinte años. Ahora tenía treinta y seis.

Nos sentamos en el porche de la entrada a fumar según lo que nos dictaba el ánimo. Ver a Buffalo-Catherine era como ver a una doctora en acción. O a un chamán. A ver, empecemos con algo para subirnos arriba de la pelota. A ver, ahora bajemos un poco, estamos muy acelerados, tú sobre todo. Toma un poco de agua. A ver, con ésta nos vamos a reír, démosle.

Ya no recuerdo de lo que hablamos con Buffalo-Catherine en ese porche. Quiero decir que de todo y de nada. Pero quiero decirlo porque no lo recuerdo. Yo ya estaba profundamente enamorado.

Lo que sí recuerdo es que Buffalo-Catherine me dijo en algún punto que era una bruja. Ah, eres medio gruñona, ¿es eso?, le pregunté yo. No, no es eso, Francés.

A lo largo de la tarde y hasta entrada la noche fueron llegando varios de sus clientes. Buffalo-Catherine los hacía pasar y nos sentábamos todos en el living, a fumar y escuchar música mientras ella iba preparando los pedidos. Sam 2 se me echaba entre las piernas y aunque su piel me daba asco yo lo acariciaba y le daba palmaditas en la cabeza.

En un momento Buffalo-Catherine se metió en la cocina a prepararse otro vodka y la mejor amiga, Sam, me dijo: no seas pavo, Francés, anda a coquetear.

Al abrir el freezer me encontré con dos viales de sangre. Pensé: quizás no salga más de aquí. Estaba borracho y el pensamiento me hizo sonreír. Era un hombre pobre y desesperado, pero también era un hombre libre y feliz.

Y esta sangre, le pregunté descuidadamente. No quería que Buffalo-Catherine pensara que yo me impresionaba con cualquier cosa.

Es del gobernador, me dijo. Un cerdo fascista republicano. Todavía no sé qué voy a hacer con ella.

Primero pensé en algún chantaje. En círculos de la droga que llegaban hasta lo más alto. En Buffalo-Catherine como parte de una red anarquista empecinada en destruir el sistema. Pero después recordé lo que había dicho sobre ser una bruja. Me imaginé algún ritual demoníaco. Recordé a un amigo que creaba sigilos a partir de kameas cabalísticos, con los que decía poder leer el futuro.

Ah, claro, le dije yo, como si también guardara la sangre de mis enemigos en el freezer del refrigerador.

Al rato la casa se fue librando de los clientes de Buffalo-Catherine. Sam se llevó a Sam 2 y se metieron en su pieza. A esas alturas yo ya fantaseaba con vivir con ellas tres y ser el hombre de la casa. El que entretiene a los clientes mientras Buffalo-Catherine prepara los paquetes con las drogas. Ordenamos el living y nos fuimos a acostar. Tenía que estar en el aeropuerto en doce horas más y estaba a siete horas manejando.

No puedo culear contigo, me dijo cuando estábamos metidos en la cama. Va a ser peor cuando te vayas.

La bruja me amaba de vuelta.

Me acordé de esa frase que un Casanova entrado en años le avienta a una mujer cuarentona que dice haberlo visto en la corte. Yo tenía quince años y usted fue mi primer amor, le confiesa ella. Ya veo, le dice él, pensativo. Usted me conoció demasiado temprano y yo a usted vengo a conocerla demasiado tarde.

La frase en realidad no se correspondía con nuestra situación. Yo estaba fofo, como Mastroianni haciendo de Casanova, pero si bien ya no era joven, tampoco era del todo viejo. Y Buffalo-Catherine, más que una cortesana, era una bruja que guardaba sangre fascista en el refrigerador. Pero la pensé de todas maneras.

Entiendo, le dije yo, simulando tristeza pero sonriendo por dentro. Nos quedamos en silencio, acostados en la cama mirándonos a los ojos, con las caras tan pegadas que se tocaban nuestras frentes. Yo sentía la mía sudada y podía olerle las axilas a Buffalo-Catherine.

Llegué al aeropuerto sin contratiempos y a la hora. Nunca había visto algo así. El aeropuerto estaba completamente vacío. Los bares y las tiendas estaban cerrados. Sólo alguna gente (los republicanos fascistas, sospeché) no llevaba máscaras encima. Me puse a escribirle una carta a Buffalo-Catherine que terminé en el avión con las siguientes frases, robando el modelo de Joe Brainard:

Recuerdo el olor de tus axilas.

Recuerdo a Sam mandándome a coquetear contigo en la cocina.

Te recuerdo a ti, Buffalo-Catherine, reina de las arañas, mi bruja hermosa.

Así que estaba de vuelta en Chile. De vuelta a vivir con mis padres. No importaba, pensaba: alguna vez, alguien me amó en Buffalo.

Profesión, me preguntó el tipo de policía internacional.

Dudé un segundo.

Barman le quise decir, pero no lo hice.

Casi dije profesor, pero pensé que sonaría a poca cosa.

Me decidí por académico, pero a último momento sentí que no era del todo cierto.

Ya sé, pensé: ¿y si digo traductor?

Pero recordé que no había traducido nada que no me avergonzara.

Así que le dije: Escritor.

El tipo ni se inmutó. ¿Dirección?

21 de febrero 2021

PONY GIRLS

Denis Bell

STORMY WORKS THE LATE CROWD at PG's. Laptop Romeos, strung out space cowboys and grizzled old pecker necks too cheap to spring for the price of admission to the classier joints uptown.

Stormy performs three sets between midnight and 2:00 am, then turns tricks the rest of the night in one of the rooms upstairs. She learned the trade at the tail end of the housing bubble when she lost her day job and was spotted on the street one night by a talent scout for the Vaugns. Stormy called herself Susan back then.

Stormy lives alone in a one-bedroom flat around the corner from the club. She is divorced, with a teenage son that she's not allowed to see. Blonde wig, enhanced collagen lips and a botched boob job that brings its own world of pain. They say you can't teach an old dog new tricks but Stormy is forty-three years of age and every year grows more versatile. *I'll die in this place,* she thinks.

RESEÑA

SE REEDITA *ERÓTICA*

Antonio Herrería

ERÓTICA (Ed. Casa Vacía, Richmond, 2021) agrupa la primera colección de cuentos y viñetas de José Prats Sariol, publicada inicialmente en Cuba, en 1988. Esta reedición resalta y toma aún más fuerza al tener en cuenta los últimos acontecimientos sociales y políticos en Cuba, donde la represión y censura, alargadas por más de seis décadas, se mantienen pese a la explosión social, como recientemente han comprobado las protestas en la isla caribeña.

Erótica da fe de su actualidad al describir las mismas problemáticas existentes en la isla más de medio siglo después de su escritura; de ahí su presente valor. Si bien los cuentos radican en su mayoría en la isla de Cuba, las situaciones descritas y las críticas al sistema se asocian con unos valores de carácter universal. El propio Prats Sariol nos describe en su introducción, titulada "Nota de arqueología literaria", cómo su personaje-censor "se convertía en típico jerarca de un régimen totalitario -ruso, nicaragüense, chino, iraní...- del siglo XVIII o del XXI", en referencia a su cuento "Index Librorum Prohibitorum", escrito en 1982.

Efectivamente, estos cuentos destacan por unos valores universales que sirven de herramienta para criticar la falta de libertad en el régimen autoritario cubano, lo que conforma el *leitmotiv*. Sin embargo, este se articula generalmente de forma disimulada dentro de los textos para escapar de la propia censura que la obra critica, así como para revelar el miedo y la delación que existen en cualquier sociedad, pero que se agudizan en regímenes totalitarios.

Como los grandes textos que consiguen escapar de las cadenas editoriales en los países totalitarios, *Erótica* burló la censura del régimen a través del uso de aspectos cotidianos aparentemente inofensivos y al asociar su crítica con modelos foráneos al cubano.

La presencia de héroes nacionales, víctimas de esos mismos sistemas represores, como muestran las inclusiones o referencias a Domingo del Monte, Julián del Casal, José Martí... ayudan a enmascarar la crítica. No obstante, si *Erótica* logró burlar la censura, el autor no salió indemne de la publicación de su libro, ya que sufrió posteriores represalias, que culminarían en su destierro en el 2001, primero en México y luego en Los Estados Unidos, lo que también muestra cómo esta obra fue identificada como subversiva por el régimen.

La censura es uno de los temas recurrentes en los cuentos de *Erótica*. De entre ellos destaca "Index Librorum Prohibitorum", obra que se inspira en el índice de libros prohibidos que se instauró en España a partir de 1551 y que continuó imperando hasta principios del siglo XIX. En el cuento, localizado temporalmente en 1793, el obispo Fernando Rávano, miembro de la Academia y censor de la Inquisición, lee y condena un texto de 1246 por contravenir la Santa Fe y las buenas costumbres. La crítica al Obispo se presenta al ser éste un sagaz lector que rememora a través de las páginas eróticas del libro su propia vida disoluta con diversas mujeres y experiencias sexuales en lupanares. El doble rasero de quienes se ensalzan como adalides y guardianes de la moral social se extrapola claramente al buen lector a otras épocas y latitudes, en donde se establece una analogía entre "inquisidores y comisarios políticos".

Similitudes con el cuento anterior se encuentran en la viñeta "Academia", en donde la censura se visibiliza al ser el gran catedrático, representante de la oficialidad, quien desaliente a un joven poeta a continuar con su obra literaria, al carecer este, supuestamente, de unos valores y normas literarias que él considera imprescindibles. Es decir, los textos se tienen que circunscribir al canon imperante, y los que no se alineen con él quedan fuera de la oficialidad. Una censura impuesta de facto desde los organismos culturales que se asocian con la famosa frase de Fidel Castro a los intelectuales con la pistola en la mesa en 1961: "Dentro de La Revolución, todo; contra La Revolución nada".

Dentro de la misma temática se halla "El despachador", donde se alude a la presencia de los órganos censores, y por tanto señala una limitación en la libertad de expresión. En el texto, una joven está escribiendo un cuento para un taller literario al cual acudirá el Asesor Provincial, perteneciente al Ministerio de Cultura, y dos escritores de La Habana. La presencia de este personaje no es casual, sino que visibiliza parte de la realidad cotidiana de los grupos culturales en Cuba.

En la misma estela argumental encontramos "¿Después?", tributo al escritor cubano Julián del Casal, en donde se narra en una ficticia conversación las dudas por publicar los amoríos de la mujer del aquel entonces capitán general de la Cuba colonial, Sabas Marín, en 1888. Unas notas en cursiva posteriores al cuento muestran cómo, debido a su publicación, Julián del Casal fue cesado de su puesto de escribiente en la Intendencia General de Hacienda. El castigo sufrido por Casal se convierte en una clara analogía con quienes destapan los trapos sucios del sistema, lo mismo que le sucedió a Heberto Padilla por su poemario disidente *Fuera del* juego y a tantos otros autores cubanos de varias generaciones.

No obstante, *Erótica* es más que disidencia política. Es simultáneamente experimentación literaria, juego verbal, como es común en otras obras literarias de Prats Sariol, entre las que destaca su novela *Mariel*. La experimentación en *Érotica* se exterioriza por la presencia de metaescrituras y metalecturas, siendo los personajes principales escritores y lectores que leen diversos textos dentro del propio texto. La experimentación lúdica no se limita a los distintos niveles de lectura, sino que también se presenta en otras formas. De esta manera, "Urganda la desconocida", presenta una influencia valle-inclanista, mientras que en la viñeta "Jenjilla" se juega con las reglas gramaticales. En esta última viñeta se narra la típica situación en que una madre se queja y pretende controlar los movimientos nocturnos de un hijo que acaba de dejar atrás la pubertad. La particularidad atemporal es que carece de puntuación, lo que potencia la lectura. De forma análoga vemos "Gorda en gerundio", donde el narrador enumera, solo a través de comas, una situación en que una mujer de edad avanzada hace su paseo para hacer la cola de la compra, que aquí asociamos con las cartillas de racionamiento, la cual, para su sorpresa, brilla por su ausencia.

En "Sofrosine", "La broma", "Dos cuartillas a la orden"...., destaca la técnica del monólogo interior. Su excelente uso presenta ciertas concomitancias con *Cinco horas con Mario*, de Miguel Delibes, y *Últimas tardes con Teresa*, de Juan Marsé. No es casual que Prats Sariol escribiera el prólogo a la edición cubana de *Últimas tardes con Teresa*, así como el de *Los santos inocentes*, de Delibes.

Otros recursos de estilo parecen dejar guiños a Albert Camus, Juan Carlos Onetti y Mario Vargas Llosa; así como a los grandes cuentistas cubanos de la generación anterior a la suya: Calvert Casey, Antonio Benítez Rojo y Guillermo Cabrera Infante.

Erótica de Prats Sariol destaca por dos ejes. Uno de ellos es de suma importancia dentro del contexto sociohistórico de la Cuba actual al permitir visibilizar, a través del uso de la intrahistoria cubana, la censura, el miedo y el castigo dentro de un sistema totalitario, como han demostrado los últimos eventos en la isla caribeña. El otro, incide en el empleo de diversas técnicas narrativas, de entre las cuales sobresale el magnífico uso del monólogo interior. *Erótica* no sólo es ameno, sino que también es un libro fuerte, como diría Harold Bloom, y desde aquí recomendamos y alentamos con vehemencia su lectura.

BLUES CASTELLANO RENACE

Marcos Pico Rentería

APARECE UNA NUEVA EDICIÓN bilingüe del conocido poemario de Antonio Gamoneda *Blues Castellano* que sale a luz en 2021 bajo la editorial independiente norteamericana *Quantum Prose*. En dicha edición, titulada *Castillian Blues* (Ed. Quantum Prose, New York, 2021), aparecen nuevas planteaciones en torno a la traducción de la literatura del castellano al inglés por editoriales norteamericanas. Si bien muchas traducciones resultan ser un meticuloso trabajo de relojería, esta edición no solamente es un caso así, sino que trae consigo los treinta y dos poemas con sus tres distintas secciones, además, incluye una introducción por parte de los editores y traductores Benito del Pliego y Andrés Fisher. El preámbulo, redactado en inglés, no solo ofrece un paneo a la trayectoria del escritor, sino que se detiene en un breve estudio de la poética de Gamoneda.

El primer punto a favor de esta publicación es el reto de publicar poesía española en los Estados Unidos en una editorial independiente. Si esto no es el acto más radical de nuestro siglo, sin duda es el más vanguardista. Espero no se entienda esto en una liga hacia Filippo Tommaso Marinetti, sino que menciono una vanguardia que va en contra del mundo editorial contemporáneo publicando letras que, aparte del mundo académico, tiende a recibir muy poca atención. Recientemente la académica y escritora de origen venezolano radicada en EE.UU. Naida Saavedra comenzó a publicar textos bajo una nueva etiqueta: *#NewLatinoBoom*. En dicha etiqueta, muy concurrente en Twitter, en Facebook y en otros blogs, nos resalta la idea de que ahora es muy común escribir, leer, editar y publicar en español en el territorio al norte del Río Grande/Bravo. Aquí me gustaría interceder por el lado académico y editorial mientras acomodo a esta publicación como parte de ese *hashtag* y el trabajo de traducción que se hace en esta nueva parte del presente siglo.

Si bien lo menciona la introducción en la edición de *Quantum Prose*, la voz de Gamoneda en este poemario, es un paralelo a la música tradicionalmente afrodescendiente norteamericana, los editores mencionan la doble función, aparte de la estética, de expresar el sufrimiento y buscar su consuelo. Bien dicho pues existe esa esencia de constantes notas de tristeza y un evangelio musicalizado en los poemas de Gamoneda, incluso uno de ellos resalta sin lugar a duda este sentimiento. La forma en que el yo poético evoca un par de recuerdos, el primero a una carta que nunca llega a su destinatario y el otro por el sufrir de una perra a la cual se le flagelaba. Si bien, ambas imágenes son crudas y difíciles de conllevar, el yo poético es capaz de dar alivio en torno a la remembranza. Para efectos de ejemplos se redactan algunos versos del poema "Malos recuerdos":

> Llevo colgados de mi corazón
> los ojos de una perra y, más abajo
> una carta de madre campesina.
>
> Cuando yo tenía doce años,
> algunos días, al anochecer,
> llevábamos al sótano a una perra
> sucia y pequeña.
>
> Con un cable le dábamos y luego
> con las astillas y los hierros. (Era
> así. Era así.
>   Ella gemía,
> se arrastraba pidiendo, se orinaba,
> y nosotros la colgábamos para pegar mejor).
>
> Aquella perra iba con nosotros
> a las praderas y los cuestos. Era
> veloz y nos amaba.

La tristesa, o mejor dicho, *sadness*, se reescribe y muta al llevarse al inglés. Si bien pensamos en Harold Boom con su conocido que 'un poema no se escribe' sino que se reescribe, bien vemos lo mismo en esta traducción. No es solo trabajo de traducción lo que nos ofrecen estos jóvenes académicos, sino que es una nueva escritura del poema de Gamoneda. Las imágenes se llevan al inglés con la premura, el azogue en el pecho, y la alargada tristeza como fue en el original, se respeta en esta nueva versión haciéndose presente ese sentir que Gamoneda nos comparte en el original. Se comparten los mismos versos en su nueva versión "Bad memories":

Hanging from my heart
I carry the eyes of a dog, and downwards,
a letter from a peasant mother.

When I was twelve,
some days, at dusk,
we took a small and dirty dog
to the basement.

We hit her with a wire and then
with sticks and irons (So it
was. So it was
        She whined
and dragged begging, she pissed
and we hung her for a better beating).

That dog went along with us
to the prairies and the hills. She was
fast and loved us.

La capacidad de Gamoneda de llevarnos a esos recuerdos de arrepentimiento y vergüenza son vívidos aunque llenos de una austeridad que profundiza la sonoridad de la tristeza. La imagen de esa perra es una hipérbole a lo más puro llevado a un dolor desgarrador, aterrador, si se permite. La violencia de la vida diaria de una familia de campo la captura en unos cuantos versos que se quedan grabados como esos latigazos a la perra veloz que los amaba.

El trabajo del presente libro lleva varios puntos a favor, pues se presenta como unas versiones revisadas y después traducidas. Los editores agradecen a Antonio y a Amelia Gamoneda por su bondad y confianza depositada en ellos para hacer posible publicación. Si una novedad resaltante para los lectores de esta edición es la nueva colección cuidada por los editores y por el mismo Gamoneda. Aunque esta colección de poemas es breve, no deja de tener un gran mérito de curaduría, traducción y edición por los involucrados en este nuevo destello poético. *Quantum Prose* ha apostado en un gran libro aunado con una cuidadosa traducción que vale la pena incorporar en muchas de nuestras aulas y, por qué no, como parte importante de nuestra colección personal de libros de poesía contemporánea.

LOS DE ABAJO, AN ARABIC TRANSLATION

Salim Daniel

THE MOST CELEBRATED NOVEL of Mexican writer Mariano Azuela *Los de abajo* was published in an Arabic translation in Baghdad, Iraq, earlier in 2021 by Iraqi translator Marwan Al-Kazzaz. Azuela (1873-1952) was involved in the Mexican Revolution as a physician, and he was an eyewitness of many events during the war as a medical officer for Pancho Villa's northern division. The novel revolves mainly on survival in brutal situations resulting from the war in which many ordinary, and mostly illiterate peasants, found themselves fighting against government forces, some of which were commanded by vicious officers, forcing the revolutionaries to kill and loot to survive.

In Azuela's *Los de abajo*, Al-Kazzaz encountered expressions and idioms used in the language of the peasants in the revolutionary saga posed some difficulties, which required a meticulous research and effort on the part of the translator to find a way to clarify the concepts depicted, regardless of how trivial they might seem to an outsider. Moreover, Al-Kazzaz had to deal with the large number of names of local plants, towns and various places where the story took place.

Marwan Al-Kazzaz was born in Baghdad in 1948. He graduated from the College of Languages, University of Baghdad, in 1970 with a B.A. in Spanish. He was trained as a professional simultaneous interpreter in Madrid, Spain, from 1980-1982 and worked for the Iraqi Ministry of Culture and Information as an interpreter and translator for many years at national and international conferences before immigrating in 1997 to the United States, where he lives currently.

Al-Kazzaz has translated several works from Spanish into Arabic, including *El Túnel* by Ernesto Sabato (1987), *Lazarillo de*

Tormes, una adaptación para niños (1987), short stories by Pedro Antonio Alarcón (1990), *Pedro Páramo* by Juan Rufo (1990), *Una señora de rojo sobre fondo gris* by Miguel Delibes (1995), and *Los de abajo* by Mariano Azuela (2021).

The Arabic translation of *Los de abajo* was published by Dijla Press in Baghdad in April 2021. Al-Kazzaz has just completed his translation into Arabic of *La familia de Pascual Duarte*, a novel by Spanish Nobel laureate Camilo José Cela (1916-2002). It is expected to come out sometime in 2022.

AUTORES

Yasef Ananda (La Habana, 1975). Poeta, cineasta, periodista y traductor. Ha publicado los poemarios "Estado de Sitio" (1990), "El Manuscrito de Ananda" (1995), "La tarde elemental" (2008) y "Abril en Mayo" (2018). Tambien es co-autor del libro "Periodismo y Nación" (2013). Sus poemas han sido traducido al inglés, hindi, chino y japonés. En el 2021 fue seleccionado como "Poeta Extranjero del Año" en China. Entre sus trabajos como guionista y productor cinematográfico se destacan los filmes "Unicornio, el jardín de las frutas", primera coproducción entre India y Argentina; y "Gozar, Comer, Partir", premio Coral en el Festival Internacional del Nuevo Cine Latinoamericano.

Denis Bell is a mathematics professor and a maker of short and flash fictions. He was born a Brit and now lives in Jacksonville, Florida. Bell's scientific work has been recognized by national funding and a Research Professorship at MSRI, Berkeley. His writing has been published in *The Prague Revue, Lotus-Eater, Flash: The International Short-Short Story Magazine, Journal of Microliterature, The Maine Review, Literary Orphans* and many other print and online literary journals. A collection of his fiction, *A Box of Dreams* was published by Luchador Press in 2020 and an expanded edition is currently in the works.

Erika Bondi, PhD., is a poet, writer, researcher and translator. She has published in journals such as *Ámbitos feministas* and *Contrapuntos* among others. After working in China at Sichuan University for four years as a Lecturer of Spanish Literature and Culture, she has returned to the Americas to travel and focus on her creative writing.

Natalia Chamorro: A poet-writer living in Queens, N.Y. Her poems can be read in contemporary poetry magazines such as Low-Fi Ardentía, Nueva York Poetry Review, Las Bárbaras, among other poetry and literary magazines. Her poem "Aria", from the forthcoming book Reflejo Escaparate, was selected for the Antología Vol. 2. Feria Internacional del Libro de la Ciudad de Nueva York, 2021. Her narrative work has been published by Latin

Lover Food & Culture, First Book, and Herstory Writers Workshop. Natalia has been awarded various creative writing and humanities grants such as NY Public Humanities Grant (2021), Regional Economic Development Council/NY State Council on the Arts Fellow-Herstory Writers Workshop (2019), and the Sylvia Molloy Tuition Grant- NYU Creative Writing in Spanish (2017-2018). Natalia holds a Ph.D. in Hispanic Languages and Literature. Currently, she is a Spanish adjunct professor at NYU. Natalia's work can be read at nataliachamorro.medium.com and nataliachamorroportfolio.wor dpress.com

Irene Cooper's writings appear in *The Feminist Wire*, *phoebe*, *Utterance*, *Denver Quarterly*, *The Manifest-Station*, *The Rumpus*, *Witness*, and elsewhere. She is the author of Committal, speculative *spyfy* about family (Vegetarian Alcoholic Press 2020) and spare change: poems (FLP 2021). She lives with her people and a corgi in Oregon.

Adam Day is the author of *Left-Handed Wolf* (LSU Press, 2020), *Model of a City in Civil War* (Sarabande Books), *Badger, Apocrypha*, (Poetry Society of America) and the recipient of a PEN America Literary Award. He is the editor of the forthcoming anthology, *Divine Orphans of the Poetic Project*, from 1913 Press, and his work has appeared in *Kenyon Review, Iowa Review, American Poetry Review, Boston Review, AGNI, Missouri Review, BOMB*, and elsewhere. In 2008 he founded and continues to direct the Baltic Writing Residency, which has hosted Ottessa Moshfegh, Salvatore Scibona, Joshua Cohen, Jennifer Percy, Josh Weil, Caitilin Horrocks, and others. He is also founder and publisher of the arts and culture magazine, *Action, Spectacle.*

Francisco Díaz Klaassen (Santiago, 1984) es autor de las novelas *Antología del cuento nuevo chileno* (2009), *El hombre sin acción* (2011, Premio Roberto Bolaño), *La hora más corta* (2016), *En la colina* (2019), y el libro de cuentos *Cuando éramos jóvenes* (2012). Trabaja como profesor de literatura inglesa en la Pontificia Universidad Católica de Chile. En 2011 fue seleccionado por la Feria del Libro de Guadalajara como uno de los 25 Secretos Mejor Guardados de Latinoamérica.

Tim Fitts is the author of two collections of short stories, *Hypothermia* (MadHat Press 2017) and *Go Home and Cry for Yourselves* (Xavier Review Press 2017). His flash fiction has previously appeared in *Contrapuntos*, *Boulevard*, *The Baltimore Review*, *Best Microfiction 2020*, *Shenandoah*, among many others.

Consuelo Hernández is a Colombian American poet, literary critic, and worldwide traveler. She has published several poetry collections: *Wake of Chance | Estela del azar* (2021), *Mi reino sin orillas* (2016), *Poems from Debris and Ashes | Poemas de escombros y cenizas* (2006), *Manual de peregrina* (2003), *Solo de violín. Poemario para músicos y pintores* (1997), *Voces de la soledad* (1982), *El tren de la muerte* (Chapbook, 2018), and the short collection *Polifonía sobre rieles* (2011). She also has written numerous articles on Latin American literature and two scholarly books: *Voces y perspectivas en la poesía latinoamericana del siglo XX* (2009), and *Álvaro Mutis: Una estética del deterioro* (1996).

Antonio Herrería es académico y escritor. Se doctoró en literatura española en la Universidad Estatal de Arizona. Ha escrito múltiples artículos y reseñas en revistas literarias tanto de literatura contemporánea como del modernismo. Entre otros proyectos, es miembro del equipo editorial de la Biblioteca Antológica; una biblioteca abierta al público con las principales obras literarias en español divididas por periodos y geografías.

Colin Ian Jeffery is an established English poet and novelist with world-wide reputation, his books can be purchased from Amazon and all good bookshops. He was seven, a choirboy, when he became entranced by poetry after hearing the twenty-third psalm. The beauty of the words struck his soul like lightning and his Muse began to sing. He then found poetry was being read on the BBC radio Home Service and would listen in awe and delight to such poets as Dylan Thomas, John Betjeman, and Ted Hughes.

R. J. Keeler was born in St. Paul, Minnesota, and grew up in the jungles of Colombia. He holds a BS in Mathematics from North Carolina State University, an MS in Computer Science from the

University of North Carolina-Chapel Hill, an MBA from the University of California at Los Angeles, and a Certificate in Poetry from the University of Washington. An Honorman in the U.S. Naval Submarine School, he was Submarine Service (SS) qualified. He is a recipient of the Vietnam Service Medal, Honorable Discharge, and a Whiting Foundation Experimental Grant. He is a member of IEEE (technological society), AAAS (scientific society), and the Academy of American Poets. A former Boeing engineer.

Sreekanth Kopuri is an Indian English poet from Machilipatnam – a colony – India. He was an alumni Writer in Residence, at *Strange Days Books* Greece. He recited his poetry and presented his research papers in many countries. His poems and research articles were widely published in journals like *Heartland Review*, *Nebraska Writers Guild*, *Poetry Centre San Jose*, *Underground Writers Association*, *Word Fountain*, *A New Ulster*, to mention a few. His book *Poems of the Void* was the finalist for the EYELANDS BOOKS AWARD. Kopuri is presently an independent research scholar in Contemporary Poetry, silence, and Holocaust poetry. He lives in his hometown Machilipatnam with his mother teaching and writing.

Dave Lordan is an Irish poet whose latest collection is *Medium* (Front Line Press, 2020). Back To Normal, a jointly authored collection with Karl Parkinson, is forthcoming in 2021. The Spanish translation of his experimental fiction collection *First Book of Frags* is about to be published in Chile by Los Perros Romanticos. He works as a literary mentor & community educator. Contact him at dlordan@hotmail.com and find him at www.davelordan.com & as Dave Lordan on Spotify & Band Camp.

John Madera is a Puerto Rican writer. His fiction may be found in *Conjunctions*, *The &Now Awards 2: The Best Innovative Writing*, and elsewhere. His nonfiction may be found in *American Book Review*, *Bookforum*, *Rain Taxi: Review of Books*, *The Believer*, and elsewhere. Recipient of an MFA in Literary Arts from Brown University, Madera lives in New York City, where he edits *Big Other* and runs Rhizomatic: Publicity for Small Presses with Big Ideas.

Ewa Mazierska is historian of film and popular music, who writes short stories in her spare time. She published over twenty of them in *The Longshot Island, The Adelaide Magazine, The Fiction Pool, Literally Stories, Ragazine, BlazeVox, Red Fez, Away, The Bangalore Review, Shark Reef* and *Mystery Tribune*, among others. Ewa is a Pushcart nominee and her stories were shortlisted in several competitions. She was born in Poland, but lives in Lancashire, UK.

Jeanne Morel is the author of the chapbooks "I See My Way to Some Partial Results" (Ravenna Press), "Jackpot" (Bottlecap Press), and "That Crossing Is Not Automatic" (Tarpaulin Sky Press). Her poem "Loss & Other Forms of Death" won the 2021 Fugue Poetry Prize. Her poems have been published in the United States, England, Hong Kong, and India. Jeanne holds an MFA in Creative Writing from Pacific University. She lives in Seattle where she teaches writing and is a gallery guide at the Frye Art Museum.

Claudia Novillo estudió en el Colegio Rosa de Jesús Cordero (Mejor egresada, medalla de oro). Habla inglés a nivel TOEFL. Obtuvo el diploma DELF B2 y el C1 en francés. Es Psicóloga de la Universidad de Cuenca y es Abogada de la UTPL. Tiene una maestría en Psicología Cognitiva de la Universidad de Cuenca. Fue ganadora del 3er concurso a mejor proyecto de investigación de la Universidad de Cuenca. Obtuvo una beca del SENESCYT (Secretaria Nacional de Educación del Ecuador), para un postgrado: Políticas Públicas, University of Queensland Australia. Tiene un postgrado en Comercio Exterior en la Universidad Rey Juan Carlos de España. Ha estudiado diseño gráfico en el Instituto de Artes de la Universidad de California.

Lucía Orellana Damacela (Guayaquil, Ecuador) ha publicado los poemarios *InHERent (*2020), *Longevity River* (2019), *Sea of Rocks* (2018), y *Life Lines* (2018), ganador del concurso literario "The Bitchin Kitsch". Sus trabajos de poesía, relato, y traducciones en inglés y en español han aparecido en antologías y revistas literarias en más de una docena de países. Algunas de las publicaciones que han incluido recientemente los trabajos de Lucía son: *PANK, Tin House Online, Carve, The Bitter Oleander, The Acentos Review,* y en la antología *Tales of Two Cities: Singapore and Hong Kong*, entre otras. Lucía obtuvo un doctorado en psicología social de Loyola University Chicago, ha sido docente de la Universidad Católica de Guayaquil, y tiene una maestría en escritura creativa en español de New York University, donde da clases en el departamento de Español y Portugués. Ha participado en lecturas y festivales literarios en Indonesia, Singapur, y Nueva York, incluidos *The Americas Poetry Festival of New York* y la *Feria Internacional del Libro de Nueva York en 2019*. Lucía ejercita su minimalismo en Twitter como @lucyda, y mantiene un blog en https://notesfromlucia.wordpress.com.

Marcos Pico Rentería (México, 1981). Profesor asistente de español en *Defense Language Institute*. Su investigación se centra en literatura latinoamericana, principalmente en torno al desarrollo del cuento y ensayo en la producción mexicana de la segunda mitad del siglo XX y comienzos del XXI. Varios de sus cuentos, entrevistas, artículos y poemas han aparecido en revistas literarias y académicas como *Conexos, La Santa Crítica, Revista Crítica, Nuestra Aparente Rendición, Eñe: Revista para leer, Vozed, Digo.palabra.txt, Confluencia*, Caleidoscopio, Campos de Plumas, Carátula y en antologías como *Alebrije de palabras* (BUAP, 2013), *Pelota Jara* (2014), *Testigos de Ausencias* (2018), *Hostos Review* (2019) entre otras.

Ellen Sander was a pioneering New York rock journalist. Trips: Rock Life in the Sixties was reissued in an augmented edition, by Dover Publications. She incubated her poetry in Bolinas, California in the seventies, and her chapbook. Hawthorne, a House in Bolinas, published by Finishing Line Press, is her homage to those poets and those times. After a stint in Los Angeles, she was an editor at Women of China magazine in Beijing in 2005, having taught English in both Xiamen and Beijing. She was the Poet Laureate of Belfast, Maine in 2013 and 2014, where she lives today, and hosts a quirky poetry radio program on WBFY the local low-wattage radio station. Her next poetry chapbook, *Aquifer* will be published by Red Bird Chapbooks.

J. J. Steinfeld is a Canadian poet, fiction writer, and playwright J. J. Steinfeld lives on Prince Edward Island, where he is patiently waiting for Godot's arrival and a phone call from Kafka. While waiting, he has published twenty-two books, including *Identity Dreams and Memory Sounds* (Poetry, Ekstasis Editions, 2014), *Madhouses in Heaven, Castles in Hell* (Stories, Ekstasis Editions, 2015), *An Unauthorized Biography of Being* (Stories, Ekstasis Editions, 2016), *Absurdity, Woe Is Me, Glory Be* (Poetry, Guernica Editions, 2017), *A Visit to the Kafka Café* (Poetry, Ekstasis Editions, 2018), *Gregor Samsa Was Never in The Beatles* (Stories, Ekstasis Editions, 2019), *Morning Bafflement and Timeless Puzzlement* (Poetry, Ekstasis Editions, 2020), and *Somewhat Absurd, Somehow Existential* (Poetry, Guernica Editions, 2021)

Rodrigo Toscano is a poet and essayist based in New Orleans. He is the author of ten books of poetry. Forthcoming in 2021 is *The Charm & The Dread* (Fence Books). His previous books include *In Range, Explosion Rocks Springfield, Deck of Deeds, Collapsible Poetics Theater* (a National Poetry Series selection), *To Leveling Swerve, Platform, Partisans,* and *The Disparities.* His poetry has appeared in over 20 anthologies, including, *Voices Without Borders, Diasporic Avant Gardes, Imagined Theatres, In the Criminal's Cabinet, Earth Bound,* and *Best American Poetry.* Toscano has received a New York State Fellowship in Poetry. He won the Edwin Markham 2019 prize for poetry. His works have been translated into French, Dutch, Italian, German, Portuguese, Norwegian and Catalan. He works for the Labor Institute in conjunction with the United Steelworkers, the National Institute for Environmental Health Science, Communication Workers of America, National Day Laborers Organizing Network, and northwest tribes (Umatilla, Cayuse, Yakima, Nez Perce) working on educational / training projects that involve environmental and labor justice, health & safety culture transformation.

Laura Andrea Vázquez López es una escritora de poesía y ficciones original de Carolina, Puerto Rico. Su trabajo se puede leer en *Pussy Magic, Rio Grande Review* y *Acentos Review.* Actualmente cursa una maestría en escritura creativa en la Universidad de Texas en El Paso.

DIGITUS INDIE PUBLISHERS
www.digitusindie.com
EDITORES INDEPENDIENTES